PER MERTESACKER

BFG

BIG FRIENDLY GERMAN
MY AUTOBIOGRAPHY

WITH RAPHAEL HONIGSTEIN

TRANSLATED FROM THE GERMAN BY CEYLAN HUSSEIN

PER MERTESACKER

BFG

BIG FRIENDLY GERMAN
MY AUTOBIOGRAPHY

WITH RAPHAEL HONIGSTEIN

TRANSLATED FROM THE GERMAN BY CEYLAN HUSSEIN

deCoubertin
B O O K S

First published as a hardback by deCoubertin Books Ltd in 2019.

First Edition

deCoubertin Books, 46b Jamaica Street, Baltic Triangle, Liverpool, L1 0AF.
www.decoubertin.co.uk

ISBN: 9781909245938

A CIP catalogue record for this book is available from the British Library.

Cover design by Leslie Priestley.

Typeset by Thomas Regan | Milkyone Creative

Printed and bound by Replika Press Pvt. Ltd.

CONTENTS

THE END

WHEN IT STARTED, I WAS PLAYING FOR HANNOVER
Under-15s. I was fifteen years old and shooting skywards, with
terrible growing pains; my left knee was particularly bad. My
parents took me to a few specialists, but all said the same thing:
'There's not much we can do.' Nobody knew where the pain
was coming from or what it meant. Nobody knew if or when it
would pass. Every day, I was in pain. Every day, I took countless
pills and I was unable to train or play for almost a year. Every
now and again, I would give it a go, but I just couldn't do it. I
no longer even made it onto the pitch. The club said, 'The boy

can't hack it. He's not that talented anyway, and to top it all off, he's now growing in a hurry. He's too tall; his gears aren't working properly.' My coach at the time told me, 'Per, this isn't going to work out. You don't have the right the physical attributes; you're not quick enough.' Even my father, who until recently had been my coach in the Under-15s, eventually arrived at the conclusion that there would be no point in my continuing to try. For him, the important thing had always been my capacity to improve in training, advancing step-by-step, but in my case there had been no progress for months on end. As a result, he had to be realistic with me. 'This is the end of the line for you,' he said one day. 'You won't make it anyway. Come on, let's forget about the whole thing.'

Had I been a boy hellbent on becoming a professional footballer, this would have been a devastating blow, almost a death sentence. Your own father no longer believes in you, even doubts you. There are questions you might ask yourself, questions like, 'Doesn't he love me anymore because of this?' For me, though, that wasn't the case. My world did not come crushing down on me in that moment, because in our family, one thing had always been clear: football was not everything.

My older brother, Denis, used to have a speech impediment that required him to attend special needs schools. My parents had always been very open about it, which impressed me immensely. Denis eventually developed amazingly: today, he has a family and a good job. Back then, I realised that there were things more important than football. At most, football was Plan B. Plan A was doing my *Abitur* – the German equivalent of A

Levels – and a sports degree in Hannover; the idea of going pro wasn't a priority – not even close to being one. For me, the most important thing was to *enjoy* playing. It was my hobby and – despite my father practically forcing me into it at the age of four – my passion. At the time, he had been managing TSV Pattensen, our hometown club. One day, he turned to me and said, 'Right, we're doing this.' Later, when he went on to be youth coach at Hannover 96, he took me along, in addition to two other Pattensen players, both of whom were better than me. I was only twelve; there was no way I would have done that on my own. I was a mere afterthought, and I realised quickly that others were more talented than me. I was not being hyped and was never made the centre of attention. To me, it was clear that at a certain point, everything was going to be over, which would be perfectly all right. Hence, when the pain arrived, I thought that that point had been reached. Dad and my coach were simply saying out loud what I had known for myself all along.

I wasn't angry. Like my parents, I had accepted the fact of the matter: I would simply have to go down another path. There was no urge to prove anything to anyone, or to prove that they were wrong about me. My dream of becoming a professional footballer hadn't been destroyed: I had never had it.

1

PATTENSEN

HAVE YOU EVER HEARD OF PATTENSEN? A SMALL town south of Hannover with eight thousand residents, twelve thousand if you count the surrounding villages. It's a rural area, where everything is within walking distance: school, sports ground, public swimming pool, football club, tennis court. Friends everywhere. Storybook, almost.

'Pattensen, Peine, Paris,' was a popular slogan in school, which is to say Pattensen was hard to top. It was, too: everything you needed was right outside your front door, in a prosperous area. And Hannover was only a thirty-minute bus ride away. My parents were involved in several sports clubs: Mum led Nordic walking and gymnastics classes; Dad was a cross-country skier, footballer, and eventually manager. Both were — and still are — utterly crazy about sports. And make no mistake, we three boys — Denis, three years my senior, Timo, three years younger, and me — definitely sensed that. Every Sunday at ten or eleven o'clock in the morning, a mandatory three-mile run was scheduled for the whole family: past the sewage plant, into the woods, and out again. We would run in all weather; no exceptions, no excuses. It was part of our upbringing. To this day, my father gets up early and does his laps at a speed which many are unable to match. We were very much made aware of the benefits of treating your body well and going through life healthily thanks to sport and activity. There was even a sauna in our house.

I was four years old when I joined my first football club. Dad had created an Under-7s side at TSV Pattensen. He coached all of us: me and my brothers. Family legend has it that my introduction actually took place in Spain, which, probably, is where I got my outstanding technique. On holiday in Menorca, Dad had thrown a ball at my feet and noted, 'Aha, the boy can play.' I can barely have been three years old.

Once a week, I had football practice, later followed by tennis and table tennis. For a while, I used to go roller skating after primary school, too, as it was the cool thing to do at the time. Without my parents' unwavering support, I would never have been able to do as much sport as I did. I will always be grateful for that, because it opened so many doors for me — doors which later on would have to be quite tall indeed.

Work had brought my father to Pattensen. He had accepted a position as lecturer at Hannover's savings bank academy. He liked the town. It combined the countryside with a good transport connection. Like my mother, my father was raised in the Harz. The Harz is a mountain range in Germany, and part of its rugged terrain extends across Lower Saxony. He is from Wildemann, she from Sankt Andreasberg; villages which are only thirty minutes apart. My brother and I actually nearly never came to be: by his own admission, my father messed up when he was a young man and, although we never found out exactly how, it was enough for Mum not to want to see him anymore. She took him back though; my dad had been lucky — just like the rest of us.

Dad is an only child, but my mother has ten siblings. At the last count, I had thirty cousins, 25 of them boys. While Dad appreciated that the Harz was a nice place to live, he also foresaw many people moving to the big cities, resulting in fewer jobs in the local area. For this reason, he continued his education, which included studying in Bonn and a lot of reading in general. Next, he decided to relocate and start a family with Mum. Neither of them wanted to hide themselves away in their new community but instead contribute to it actively. No matter the subject, they got involved: for them, team sport was a quick way to integrate.

My brothers and I were enthusiastic eaters; our favourite meal was tomato soup with pasta followed by apple cake. What's more, we were growing extremely fast. There was a lot to do for Mum, who had to top up supplies constantly: every other day, she would come home with a full shopping trolley. If you were late, though… well, tough luck: the others would have already scoffed the lot. During the holidays, my brothers and I were often garrisoned at my dad's parents' in Wildemann. Their house was at the foot of a mountain, where snow fell heavily in the winter. We would spend hours at a time playing five-a-side on a small pitch with a big group of friends and cousins. Today, locals will tell my father, 'Of course Per got to where he is now, with all the time he used to spend playing football down here!'

In the summer, we would participate in the village sports day and go into the forest to build a wooden hut, assisted by Grandad Michael, a qualified engineer. He had come back from the war with countless scars on his face and upper body, inflicted by pieces of shrapnel. As a little boy, I had always been fascinated and intrigued by this, but he would never talk about it. At Easter, we would collect twigs, run a tree trunk into the ground, and surround it with fir for the bonfire. It was a spectacle: every year, four bonfires were set up. Building and experiencing things together enriched our childhood; it was a ritual that shaped us — my friends, my brothers, and me. It was a tranquil time. Camaraderie was paramount, as well as the idea of occupying yourself with simple things — a completely different kind of life to today's generation. Everyone is staring at their phones, submerged in a social media world that is not really social at all but extremely isolated. Often, digital networks are pseudo networks: technology tends to separate people from each other rather than unite them. Grandad Michael, originally from the Rhineland, was Catholic. Around the River Rhine, Mertesacker is quite a common name; it is derived from Saint Martin of Tours: 'Mertesacker' essentially means Martins Acker — Martin's field.

After the war, Grandad Michael and Granny Irmgard lived a modest life. My father still remembers how he used to bring his father food in a milk churn; on Saturdays, Mett – pork mincemeat eaten raw – served on a bun was a highlight. There was no television or telephone in the house: children played in the woods or in the street, as there were no recreational facilities back then either. Grandad had a Rhineland sense of humour that followed him to the Harz. He laughed a lot and took a relaxed view of most things. To him, the glass was always half full, never half empty. He was a loyal member of the choir and enjoyed celebrations, something that was passed on to my dad and me. 'Always be positive. Let things slide once in a while, have fun with others — you'll see the world in a different light. It'll take you much further than moping about and pondering all the things that could be better.' That was his attitude. He always cheered us on in everything we did but especially when it came to sport.

Grandad loved watching the Tour de France on TV. He was involved passionately with the local sports club, TSG Wildemann, helping to build the clubhouse and refereeing their games. When my father was a little boy, the two of them used to listen to the football on the radio, and Dad had to put all results into a notebook. Today, he believes that his knack for numbers originated there. Dad loves statistics: who played where, who played when, who scored the goals. World Cups, European Championships, the Olympics — he has it all on standby, saved on the hard drive between his ears. He really is a walking book: he doesn't need a mobile, because he knows every phone number by heart.

Dad and Grandad would drive to matches Grandad was officiating, and sometimes, they would go to Braunschweig to watch a game together, including the play-offs that still existed back then before the creation of the Bundesliga in 1963. At this time there were five regional top flights, with Braunschweig playing in the Oberliga Nord. Each year the winner and runner-up of the league would compete with the best teams from the other four regional leagues for the German Championship at the end of the season. After finishing runners-up in the 1957/58 campaign, Braunschweig got their opportunity and faced Karlsruher SC, Schalke 04 and Tennis Borussia Berlin, though they did not make it through to the final. Later they attended Eintracht Braunschweig's first-ever Bundesliga match, a 1-0 win over Preußen Münster in the summer of 1963. It roused my father's ambition and his love for football. As a cross-country skier, he started in several championships and spent the summer months playing football at non-league level for TuSpo Petershütte and Sportfreunde Ricklingen. He says he could run a lot and could cover every blade of grass, but just not quickly enough. After moving to Hannover, he studied for his coaching badges. Shortly before I went professional at Hannover 96, Grandad Michael passed away. I believe and hope that somehow he was able to see everything, but it would of course have been nicer had he experienced it. In my youth, he had followed my athletic career very closely, collecting all the newspaper clippings that mentioned me or my teams. Granny Irmgard continued this tradition and even witnessed my jump into Hannover's first team. When I was very little and no one could have known that I would one day go professional, she had been the one to set me straight: 'Bayern are a no-go. Don't you dare become a Bayern fan. I won't have that strip in my home.'

I had a special relationship with both of them, but Granny Erika, my mother's mother, was very loving towards us, too. After all, if someone gives birth to that many children, their heart must be in the right place. Her husband had died young — jaundice — but she still laughed a lot and was unfailingly optimistic. Even in old age, when she lost a leg due to arterial disease, she didn't lose any of her strength nor the courage to continue living contently; her willpower was amazing. On Erika's birthday, 23 December, the entire family always congregated in the Harz. To this day, the annual walk between Christmas and New Year still happens: a hike is followed by a gathering in a pub, where someone will accompany the singing on an accordion. I was lucky enough to grow up with this tradition because the generation before mine had started it, but who keeps up something similar nowadays? Chatting to people about the custom, especially in football, I'm often met with blank stares. 'Come again? What do you mean, you go hiking and singing with your whole family?'

I was cut off from this world for a few years following my transfer to Arsenal in the summer of 2011, because we would keep playing throughout Christmas and I would only get a few days off in January, if at all. As a result, the significance of our family get-together only became clear to me when I could no longer take part. It was a shock the first time around: to me, it felt like I'd let down my family, and with it, everything we'd built up together over the years. Before I knew it, I spent three days in bed, ill and unsettled. Now I'm retired, I look forward to reviving the tradition. In the meantime, my parents and brothers have been worthy substitutes. Right now, with fewer people living in and around the Harz and the local population beginning to age, it's important to keep up our connection to our home: once a year, the family spends a weekend in a hostel in Sankt Andreasberg. Not everyone can make it every year — some aren't as keen, others are otherwise engaged — but it's still nice seeing your relatives, telling each other about your lives, and developing an interest in people within the family. Every year, this ritual needs active planning and organising, or it would end up being cancelled and, presumably, we would eventually lose touch altogether. I think we should be quite proud of ourselves for managing to keep the extended family together, which, especially since the grandparents have passed, is no easy feat.

To this day, my big brother still visits the Harz for Easter to light the bonfire, and we all tend to our grandparents' graves in Wildemann. My parents see to it that Grandma and Grandad's house remains in good condition. We've filled it with furniture from my old Bremen flat to keep it homely and, to keep it from standing empty, we have family members and guests stay there as often as possible over Christmas. To me, the bond to your family's home isn't just an idea or a feeling; it's something you need in order to live. When my wife and I leave London with the kids, exchanging the grey for the beauty of the Harz with its mountains and valleys, it warms our heart. Sometimes, we'll spend holidays there with friends and their families, who join us on tours across gorgeous hiking trails and running tracks, breathing a completely different kind of air. Celebrating life events in places we grew up, places close to our hearts, also renews that feeling of togetherness: Ulrike and I got married at Marienburg Castle near Pattensen, while Oscar, our second son, was baptised in Wildemann.

Like family relations, friendships need maintaining too — especially long-distance ones — but I'm lucky to be very close to many of my old mates. In professional football, you can count your real friends on the fingers of one hand. You could sit next to someone in the dressing room for years without really knowing them. Everyone tends to do their own thing outside of matches and training now; that's just the way the industry has gone. As much as I've seen of the world during my career, I'm very glad to have had family and friends who always knew exactly who I was underneath the shirt and who kept me grounded throughout; rather than tell us not to forget our roots, our parents implicitly taught us not to.

Football properly started late in the summer of 1989, just before my fifth birthday, when I played my first league game with Denis. There were a dozen of us, boys and girls, in mismatched kits. Other teams in our age bracket were already familiar with the code and, as a result, were better organised. We, on the other hand, lost a lot of games but didn't let that spoil the fun. From day one, I played at the back, just in front of the goalkeeper. Most kids tend to run after the ball, trying to score, but that — for reasons I can't quite explain myself — never appealed to me. 'Go on, son,' my dad used to say, 'get involved a bit, jeez!' But no, I wasn't interested; I didn't want to be a hero. I wanted to protect the defence, to cover my teammates' backs. Let the others shine, let them celebrate their goals. I was happy at the back, watching out for danger. That has never changed.

Dad was very emotional when it came to football: he'd shout at the referee and raise his voice in the dressing rooms. I, however, took after my mother: I was placid, quiet, reserved on the pitch. Emotional outbursts weren't my thing — according to Dad, you could hardly ever tell the match result just from looking at my face. I only had one position, so I could hardly be described as versatile, but on the other hand, I was two-footed, quite good at reading the game, and my positional play was decent. After all, when you've had a million shots coming at you, you eventually familiarise yourself with every flight path and so know exactly where to stand. I was good in the air, too, thanks to Dad and my brothers. At the public pool and during every holiday, the four of us would get in the water with a beach ball, trying to outdo each other with headers: fifty, sixty, seventy; over time, it made a difference. While my first year with TSG didn't go all that well, the second saw us assemble a passable squad, completed with a few players from town. Our team grew in strength thanks to Dad, who invested a lot of his time and coached us with diligence: elsewhere, kids were still dribbling past cones, but Dad was teaching us proper forms of play. Often, my friends and I would go to the local lido, where there was a small pitch. Anyone who could kick a ball was instantly taken in by the older kids: 'Go on, then, where do you play?' Telling them I played for Pattensen's Under-11s gave me a feeling of immense pride. I was playing tennis and table tennis on the side, but it was football that I enjoyed most and which had the greatest effect on my self-worth. Dad did a lot to further my development: for hours, he'd have me do keepy-uppies with my weaker left foot. Due to my considerable height, I was a step ahead of kids my own age and able to skip several years. From Under-9s to Under-13s, we were constantly in the league's top positions, becoming regional champions, and even winning matches against Hannover 96's youth teams. These days, many of my former teammates are part of Pattensen's veteran squad, and they're badgering me to join them. They might have to wait a few years.

Our results meant Hannover soon started paying attention to us: 'Why are they so strong? Who's managing them?' The story of the surprisingly successful small-town club got around quickly, which resulted in Dad, together with an assistant coach, taking over the second team of Hannover's Under-13s in 1995, filling two jobs. In addition, there was a personal connection: my teammate Florian Gramann's father was treasurer at Hannover, so Florian, Markus Weck and I transferred to the team my dad was now managing. At the time, the other two were ahead of me in their development and were believed to be the greater talents. Really, I basically just slipped in alongside them. Leaving Pattensen for Hannover was considered a minor sensation in the area: everyone in the town had their own – unfiltered – opinion and was sure to make it known to everyone else. In 2015, a local journalist approached me with an apology for writing me off at the time. He's on staff for the *Leine Nachrichten*, the regional section of the *Hannoversche Allgemeine*, covering Pattensen, Hemmingen, and Saarstedt. 'Wants to play football, does he?' the piece had said, 'He should stick to swimming.' An error of judgement, apparently.

At twelve years old, I probably wouldn't have gone to Hannover on my own, so being part of a trio made the decision easier. Soon, it transpired that the other two definitely had what it took; Markus in particular was very, very good. He was immediately bumped up to the Under-15s, was always a year above me and was always better, continually overshadowing me. They thought he was more likely to make it. In time, though, his body gave up on him, and he developed severe back pain. Luckily, Markus was always very good in school and had sensible parents, so he was well equipped for a life away from professional football. Eventually, he became an apprentice in banking. His story showed me, for the first time ever, the volatile nature of this sport: the greatest talent I knew had suddenly fallen off the map.

While I was an avid collector of Panini stickers, I didn't really have a role model. I liked Ingo Anderbrügge, an attacking midfielder with Dortmund and Schalke through the late 1980s and 1990s, for his powerful left foot and also for the way I saw him behave at the end of a Schalke friendly in the Hannover borough of Ricklingen. After the final whistle, Anderbrügge and his teammates were signing autographs for the fans. I managed to get one too, and that left a lasting impression on me. From that day, I had a soft spot for Schalke, but Hannover remained, of course, my number one. Equipped with a club ID, youth players were allowed to sit on a wooden bench underneath the stands in the — back then — venerable and quite spacious Niedersachsenstadion. What a highlight that was.

At times, I'd be standing in block H31 with my Pattensen

friends; at others, I was a ballboy high-fiving players in the tunnel. Standing on the touchline was something very special; it made me feel like I really belonged, like I was part of the club. Back then, Hannover played in the second division before being relegated to the third in 1996, just when they were celebrating their one-hundredth anniversary. When they hosted Energie Cottbus under floodlights in the play-offs for promotion back to the second division a year later, I watched them from the stands: the first leg was a goalless draw, the second a 1-3 defeat in Cottbus. As a result of this setback, Hannover were plunged into deep financial trouble. The club's very existence was at stake. Still, that lack of money indirectly gave a chance to a new generation of players. Fabian Ernst, Gerald Asamoah, and Sebastian Kehl all moved up the from the Under-19s and ultimately helped the club return to the second division.

Of course, 1996 was also England's turn to host the Euros. It was the first tournament I was fully aware of. I vividly remember the penalty shootout in the semi-final: Gareth Southgate, the current England manager, stepped up for the deciding effort but had his shot saved by Andy Köpke. I still remember the final against the Czech Republic, too: it was Oliver Bierhoff's Golden Goal that famously brought the trophy home to Germany. My most poignant memory of football on TV, however, was Schalke's UEFA Cup final against Inter a year later: I was allowed to stay up late and, after Schalke's win, flung myself into my father's arms.

Some years later, my family and I drove to England by car to visit my aunt Ute in Plymouth. Our summer holiday that year was spent in London, where my father ordered each member of the family to take home a football strip (apart from Mum, who was excused). Timo, my little brother, decided on Manchester United, Denis went for Aston Villa, and my father for Ipswich Town. My choice was a red top with white sleeves and the letters JVC on the front: Arsenal. That day, the Gunners became my English club. Every year for our birthdays, we were allowed to wish for a new strip. Timo and I stuck with Manchester and Arsenal; we both loved football and were now adding 'our' Premier League sides to the sibling rivalry. In the late 90s and early 2000s, the two clubs usually competed for the league title between themselves. Once a week, German TV channel DSF would broadcast a show called 'La Ola', giving us continued access to Premier League highlights and keeping us in the loop. Outside of school and sport, we spent our time on the PC: NHL 98, NBA Live, and so on. My older brother was also very much into fantasy: he owned a board game called *Das Schwarze Auge* and a computer game called 'Might and Magic'. The latter involved four characters on a journey across the landscape: a druid, a cleric, a knight, and an archer in search of caves filled with various kinds of monsters.

Meanwhile, the time had come for me to progress to sixth-form level. My school was a comprehensive with only a small A-level class — only fifteen to twenty students — but my parents didn't want me to leave my surroundings, so I stayed put. A-level students at my school were considered swots and accused of thinking they were better than everyone else. The others would very much make you feel like an outsider, especially during class.

They would stand around in their own little smokers' groups, which you generally passed without saying a word. On principle, you didn't get invited to any of the parties. Similarly, the Old Town festival and marksmen's festival never gave you the feeling of real belonging. If, at that age, you're not involved with everyone and everything, you tend to be left out automatically anyway. In addition, there was the sporting rivalry, organised in the form of tournaments spanning several schools: our squad was excellent at everything from basketball and handball to football and beach volleyball. My feeling for the ball, whatever its shape and size, naturally meant I was at the helm. For years, we dominated and were practically unbeatable, which meant people hated us: you couldn't cross the yard without being heckled. Where some managed to gain acceptance with the popular crowd by smoking cigarettes or marijuana, this wasn't an option for me, so I was forced to stick with my kind. I had two really close friends at school.

We could never be bothered to spend our breaks in the yard; instead, we'd play cards and eat our packed lunches while listening to Walkmans. My first CD was a Die Prinzen album, but that was quickly replaced by Bob Marley, and Bob Marley only. Back then, his music was the soundtrack to our lives. I only found out later that Marley was a big football fan. The first thing people tend to associate with him, of course, is weed ('Stoner music, that's what it is!'), but we were never tempted. Instead, we wanted to understand his lyrics and the stories behind them: who were those songs aimed at? What was their context? My mates and I engaged extensively with the lyrics and soon realised that, contrary to popular belief, they were actually about something completely different. Take 'No Woman, No Cry', for example — a swansong for love, right? Wrong. The song deals with political tensions in Marley's hometown, his promise to return to his wife, and the hope that everything would be fine before long. Hip-Hop was big with us, too: on a foreign exchange, we went to Hastings and London, where I bought a Wu-Tang Clan CD. Our teacher told us to take a tour of the capital, but as boys of fifteen and sixteen, we didn't give museums and Big Ben a second's thought. Instead, we went to the arcades at Piccadilly Circus and played pinball and laser tag for five straight hours. Not until two decades later did I finally catch up with the sightseeing. Bob Marley also featured prominently in my childhood bedroom: the walls were decorated with a giant Jamaica flag and a picture of his face, next to a poster of Anna Kournikova and Hannover's cup-winning side of 1992. I wasn't the tidiest boy, which meant that my father swore repeatedly whenever he came into my room and saw the mess on the floor. '*Meine Fresse!* Every time I come in here, I'm only one step away from a torn ligament!' According to him, my way of cleaning amounted to little more than piling things on top of each other in the middle of the room.

Remarkably, once I progressed at Hannover, some of the people who wouldn't give me the time of day at school promptly changed their minds. Suddenly I was everyone's best mate: 'You haven't got a spare ticket, have you?' For me, realising that *who* you were could so quickly be eclipsed by *what* you were was a strange experience. Suddenly, my status had changed, as had people's perception of me. But I knew exactly where my roots lay, who my friends were, and who I was — and wasn't — concerned with: where had they been before? Before my progress, they didn't have a word to say to me. In the beginning, I was pleased that my father was managing a Hannover youth side: it made the transition to 'proper' football a lot easier. He did definitely push me but it never felt like it; first and foremost, I was happy to be taking part and being able to keep up. Eventually, though, rebellion took over: I didn't want Dad to train me anymore, didn't want to be in the starting XI just because the coach shared my last name. In addition, I preferred keeping football and family life strictly separate. I wanted to free myself to an extent from Dad's constant scrutiny and week-long criticism. The time had come to allow different influences onto the pitch; it was crucial to take this step towards footballing independence.

Under a new coach, I progressed to the Under-14s, and I soon found out that I had to adjust my game accordingly or risk jeopardising the team's defence, or worse, my own health. I wasn't the fastest runner, and by then I was already relatively tall, so by the time impulses had been transmitted from my brain to my feet, the ball and the opponent had long gone. One day, Under-19s coach Mirko Slomka invited some of the Under-14s for joint training, a kind of internal scouting session, if you will. After one of the older players had lifted me off my feet with a sliding tackle, I was expecting to hear the whistle, but Slomka, refusing to acknowledge the foul, allowed play to continue. I was close to tears: being booted up in the air by someone four years older, only for the manager to turn a blind eye, was beyond belief for a boy of thirteen or fourteen. The injustice of it hurt more than the kick. Not until a few years later did I understand Slomka's thought process: he had wanted to challenge the younger players, to see how they might react.

Mind you, this was the only time I was to find myself in such a situation during my youth. Early on, I developed the ability to judge and time tackles correctly: was there a chance of winning the ball properly or was I likely to commit a foul? I always tried to pass the ball before an opponent got too close, and with clarity and precision; that's a centre-half's job. Unsurprisingly, I wasn't the dribbling type. A few of the other young players tried desperately to get their coach's attention by provoking older boys and nutmegging them. It's a risky little game: some of them took a few bruises in return.

The biggest talents had already been moved up to the Under-15s. That age saw me be part of county football for the first time. In Germany, the best players from the *Länder* (the federal states across the country) get selected by their respective associations to play against each other, a kind of precursor to getting called up to the national youth team. In short, it's a big deal. I spent three days at a training camp in Barsinghausen, where the wheat was ruthlessly separated from the chaff. Markus, the boy who had left Pattensen for Hannover with me a few years before, was a permanent member of the county team. The hype started early; his parents and even grandparents attended his matches. I, on the other hand, never made it; after two camps they stopped considering me. There was no announcement; no one who took me aside to explain the situation to me gently, the invitations just stopped coming. According to my father, I wept when I realised, which usually never happened. I generally never showed any emotions after losing a match, but this hit me hard — partly because Markus had managed to cement his place in both the county team and Hannover's Under-15s. Granted, I had never been regarded as a special talent, but now, I was just a second-rate youth player. I was inferior, that's how I felt. For the first time, it occurred to me: this was it. I was done.

Whenever I went to watch the Under-15s during county tournaments, I was in awe of the level of performance. It was incredible, worlds apart from my own displays. Emmanuel Krontiris was among those starlets, scoring goal after goal with his powerful left foot. He would later sign for Tennis Borussia Berlin and started a few times for Dortmund.

This is football, I thought, standing there watching them. *These kids are going to make it.*

My time with the Under-14s was quite mediocre: I didn't stand out in any way. A few months later, when I had joined the Under-15s, I had finally reached the end of the line. Many of the boys were simply more physically developed, with thicker upper thighs, a wider torso, more strength and greater stamina. They won matches for the team, so the coaches backed them. I would see these boys in the dressing room and think I didn't stand a chance. Having my own inadequacies presented to me every other day took the fun out of the whole thing; it made me feel uncomfortable.

Then, the growth problems began. The pain in my knees was so bad that for nine months, I barely played at all. No matter how much I tried, it just wouldn't get any better. My father being Stefan Mertesacker, the man who contributed so much to the club's academy, meant that I remained an official part of the team and was still allowed to watch the first XI on match days. While I received a small portion of the respect the club showed my father, I no longer attended training — or matches, for that matter. I found myself in an interim state, a kind of limbo which was difficult to process properly: suddenly, most of my time was spent either at home or at school. It was a strange feeling. Fortunately, through my father's contacts, I was eventually introduced to Edward Kowalczuk, the first team's head of conditioning.

Kowalczuk gave specific, individual training sessions to Florian Gramann, the treasurer's son, at the county training ground by the Niedersachsenstadion. Knee problems meant that Gramann, too, was unable take part in regular training. And while I joined these weight and strength sessions, other exercises without a ball were out of the question. My father — rather bluntly — washed his hands of my playing career at the time: 'Well, professional football is off the table.' My mother's attitude was very relaxed. 'You'll finish school, then we'll take it from there.' Her calm helped me deal with the disappointment well. Fine, I told myself, I'd just take up playing again when I was ready: football could just be a hobby. I should be able to relax, seeing as there was no professional future for me anyway. I simply had to make sure I'd be able to play again *some day* — the level didn't matter.

At school, PE invariably remained my best subject. This was my father's priority, although I scraped by well enough elsewhere as well. I was consistently in the top third despite not being the most studious. Foreign languages weren't my forte (German was okay); I leaned more towards other subjects. I was a quiet type and only put up my hand if I had something of substance to say. Had I needed to study a lot in order to pass, I would've struggled — badly — but I managed fine: my progress through the years was never at risk, and my parents were never summoned to the headmaster's office. They were reassured about me doing my A*bitur*, so they let me be. At home, I didn't talk much about exams and grades: good results were presented, poorer ones withheld. Even then, I was good at holding myself to account, according to my mother. Because, all in all, school was going smoothly, my football problems didn't feel quite as dramatic as they might've done. And in any case, education always came first in our house.

In the meantime, Dad had been promoted to Head of Youth Development at Hannover. With his son unable to hack it, the situation was complicated, but Dad had an incredible knack for forging strong relationships (learning every single youth player's name, for instance) and getting people enthusiastic about things. He acquired a reputation that's still intact to this day. People trusted his judgement because he had served the club well and had opened doors for other managers. Honestly, I think I was kept on the Under-15s team as a favour to him. It wasn't much more than a nice gesture, because everyone probably thought the same thing: the boy won't make it, but let's keep him around a bit longer for his father's sake. My being granted one final stretch of necessary time was due to Dad more than anyone else. Of course, in those days, the job of youth coach was entirely voluntary rather than the highly-paid full-time position offered in modern football. Back then, people would arrive at the training ground after finishing their day job and only got their expenses paid. If that. They were idealists: in today's world, that kind of sacrifice is unimaginable.

When I joined the Under-16s, Waldemar Krause became my coach. By incredible coincidence, he was my school's caretaker and so would drive me to training every now and again, which made my life a whole lot easier. I was the very last to be added to the squad. My knees permitting, Waldemar would use me as playmaker, which really didn't suit me. I wasn't comfortable playing with my back to the opposing team's goal, and my turning circle was simply too broad.

Sometimes, my parents would drive me to training; on other occasions, I took the bus from Pattensen to either Steintor station or Hannover's central station. From there, it was a short train journey to the training ground. I used the commute for homework or studying, listening to music, or sometimes just for sleeping. In retrospect, it was something of a miracle that I never missed my stop; I would always wake up just before Pattensen. Objectively, there were more pleasant things than coming home late at night wearing dirty clothes and covered in red clay, but there was no other way. Looking back, I'd say football was a great help when it came to staying on the right track. I was definitely tempted to hang out with my mates, maybe even start smoking or drinking. At fourteen or fifteen, that seemed to happen to a lot of people. But there was football, always. Training, always. Straight after school, and then during the weekend. In any case, when away games were scheduled at Holstein Kiel or VfB Lübeck, I was generally on the road for quite some time, going back and forth during match day: I never had the chance to get any stupid ideas. 'Can't, I've got football,' was always a good excuse. Yet, it wasn't easy missing large parts of normal teenage life. When my friends were having garden parties at the weekend, I'd be on the road for hours at a time and, sometimes, that created a bit of an identity crisis.

And one of those parties very nearly threw me off course.

Thanks to Waldemar, we were allowed to do our pre-season training at school, in Pattensen, and spend the nights there, too. One day, I overheard some class mates planning a party in one of the allotments behind the school. 'Listen up, boys,' I said, 'there'll be alcohol and girls — let's get in there!' Granted, it wasn't the best idea I'd ever had: a big group of alcohol-fuelled boys *had* to result in chaos. Someone started a fight, which escalated quickly and turned into a mass brawl: Pattensen v Hannover's Under-16s. And, me, helpless in the middle. The boys who'd arranged the party eventually went to Waldemar Krause to complain about being attacked by his players. Of course, Waldemar knew at once who was responsible. 'You can go straight home,' he told me angrily, 'you're done.'

I could barely sleep that night; I was sure I'd never play for 96 again. How could I have been such an idiot? The next morning, I told Mum what had happened. She grabbed me by the collar and put me on my bike: 'We're going straight down there, and you're going to apologise. This is your fault, and you'll face the music for it.' Minutes later, I stood crying before Waldemar in the school's car park, asking for forgiveness. He considered for a moment. 'Fine. Training's at eleven.' Amnesty! But I'd learned an important lesson: small moments of stupidity can have vast consequences.

As an unfancied substitute, I certainly couldn't take any liberties. I kept growing in height and still struggled with my knees, especially the left one. On the other hand, my mind was now completely clear. The pressure of reaching a goal had disappeared, if only because I thought it was completely unrealistic. I was able to enjoy playing at Hannover, because I knew it would be over soon. 'Free our minds,' Bob Marley sings in 'Redemption Song', a song about salvation. And there I was, actually redeemed, actually free of all expectations and secret hopes.

And suddenly, from one day to the next, I was freed from my pain. My body was no longer my enemy: I was able to run and run fast. It came out of the blue. My father couldn't believe it. He saw me play and thought, 'That's not my son! What's happened to him?' All of a sudden, I was able to keep up with the team's level, both in terms of pace as well as style of play. It was a completely new sense of self-worth. Maybe it *was* my right to play, maybe I *did* belong here after all. My father didn't matter, my family background didn't matter, I was playing because I worked hard and filled my position properly. At the end of the day, it wasn't very complicated anyway, my role was well defined: win your tackles and play a simple pass to your nearest teammate. I had the whole game in front of me, but never tried to play outside my comfort zone. The urge wasn't there; instead, I simply did the job I was assigned to do as well as possible. 'Play as dry as a bone,' was the motto.

Back then, defenders followed a strict order: win the ball and pass it on — use your brains and play it neatly to your man, don't just bash it up to the front. Flawless, simple solutions with no frills: clean play was the emphasis. When I started playing county football, I was made centre-half for the first time in organised games. It was then that I noticed I wasn't lagging behind anymore. The introduction of the back four into German football was a great help, too. Waldemar was Polish and very innovative, open to new ideas that deviated from the German norm (two markers and a sweeper). Around the turn of the century, hardly any Bundesliga side was playing with a back four or zonal defence. At Pattensen, I'd still been the typical German sweeper, but Waldemar taught me the basic frameworks of a system that would become standard for us a few years later. He trained me in the essentials: where to stand; when to drop off, that is to say, when to move away from my opponent to secure the area behind them; how to support my partner; and how to move into space. Thanks to Waldemar, these things became natural to me at seventeen: he'd paved the way for my next steps.

One day, Rolf Müller, the head of conditioning at Hannover, was watching one of the Under-16s' games next to my father. 'Who's that lanky kid at the back there?' he asked. 'Well, that's my son,' my father replied. My abilities in the air were improving, so much so that every now and then I'd score with my head. When, as a reward, I was promoted to the Under-17s, Waldemar came with me. During the second half of the season in our regional league, I scored a headed goal against Osnabrück. Afterwards, my father was approached by three men, led by Harun

Arslan, who is now Jogi Löw's agent.

'That kid's good,' they said, 'has he got an agent yet?' Nowadays, it's quite natural for every seventeen-year-old to have an agent, but back then it wasn't. Not to mention that, when I was fifteen or sixteen, no one was interested in me anyway. As a result, my father, rather bemused, rejected those efforts immediately.

To my own surprise, I soon made my way into the Under-19s side. The coach, a household name, was Jürgen Stoffregen, who had been managing the first team some years before. I signed my first-ever contract. The salary was negligible: 150 Deutschmarks (around €75) a month during the first year, 300 in the second. In addition, I got a concessions card for ÜSTRA, our public transport system, to ensure my mobility. And that was it. There were no boot deals back then; you were proud to wear that one Globetrotter training kit you had, because it featured the 96 badge. Physios and coaches who were only with the club part time or came to training after their day jobs had to come up with ideas to organise a twenty percent discount with some kit supplier.

It wasn't much, but it was helpful. On public transport, there was time to do your homework, read a book, or catch up on sleep. You were on your own when it came to planning and understanding railway timetables. This may sound trivial, but things have changed over time, especially in England: Arsenal's academy, which I took charge of in the summer of 2018, currently requires that all minors be chauffeured to training by cab. I'm not allowed to give players a lift in my car the way Waldemar Krause used to, either. Personally, I find this kind of all-round care quite problematic, because it doesn't reflect reality. Instead, youth players of sixteen, seventeen get used to their bubble so fast that they forget how to read the Tube map. It goes along the lines of, 'We're worth fifty million; we're not mixing with the normal people anymore.' There's a danger some boys will end up feeling like that. The hype can get too strong.

300 Deutschmark a month – around €150. A nice bit of pocket money, nothing more. Back then, that was the signal; it meant that you'd better keep working, keep developing. Stay in school, because the whole football thing could be over in a heartbeat. In order to earn a bit on the side, I mowed our neighbours' lawn once a week. It was a lot of land and usually took me the best part of three hours. My reward? Thirty Deutschmark and some sparkling apple juice. Later on, I did two internships; one at a bank and one with an insurance company. In today's Premier League, seventeen-year-olds may sign contracts worth €100,000 a year. From that moment on, their world revolves around football: all their energy, all their attention is now focused on making it as a professional. And considering the extremely long odds, going all in is a big mistake. At 21, eighty percent of academy graduates are out on the street, empty handed. Kids of thirteen, fourteen are being pushed to neglect their education, because their parents smell the money. The pressure put on these kids is so severe that many of them develop mental health issues or suffer physical breakdowns. Of the players who joined my age group in the county squad, not a single one managed to establish themselves with the pros. For a wide variety of reasons. Some were prone to injuries, others developed too much muscle mass too soon, which might've given them a physical advantage at

the time, but ultimately lead to their actual playing potential being overrated. At seventeen, I'd left this high-carat lot behind, had pulled ahead of players who two years before would've been beyond reach. I never thought the tables could turn this quickly. I was effective, fast, and physically up to speed. Before, strikers had been too powerful and agile and I kept falling behind. But all of a sudden, I was able to keep up with the pace. There came a moment during a random match when a thought occurred to me. I had made it. Everything was working out. I couldn't believe it. Over the first five metres, I was able to react so fast that forwards couldn't get past me. When you barely need any time to react, you automatically gain a bit more time to assess the situation properly, so these split seconds are crucial. Gradually, with every situation well managed, with every match well played, I was adding self-assurance to my game.

It was a mystery to many how a boy of my height (6ft 5in) was playing football for Hannover. 'Everything he does looks so slow,' was a phrase I heard *a lot*. I did regularly finish in the top three during the sprint tests supervised by Edward Kowalczuk, though, and always jumped the highest. It was good to receive tangible reassurance, and so I enjoyed seeing those results. They did, however, surprise a fair number of people. Kowalczuk determined that my white, fast-twitch muscle tissue — relevant to sprinting — was more pronounced than its red, slow-twitch counterpart — relevant to endurance. It explained my lower-than-average results when it came to long runs, and contradicted everything people watching me did, and still do, think of me. My coordinative skills, on the other hand, were well developed, thanks to all the time spent honing them with Kowalczuk whenever my knee wouldn't let me train with the team. Lots of aerobics, lots of jumping on and off the vaulting box. While with the Under-19s, I also noticed that my fine motor skills coped well with complex tasks. After finishing our sessions with Kowalczuk, we were often given the opportunity to work with physiotherapists. It was a completely new world and really quite fascinating: all these people were willingly looking after us players in addition to their actual work assignments. Seeing this was an incentive for me, too. Training alone wasn't enough: you had to do more, go the extra mile.

At league games, I would bump into youth internationals who two years before had played on a completely different level to me. Suddenly, I was able to hold my own against players like Bremen's Alexander Ludwig. I was a key component in our Under-19s side, and finished my first season with thirty matches and a handful of goals under my belt. Quite literally a handful, too: five exactly, all of them headers. One particular goal stuck in my mind: we were trailing St. Pauli 3-2, and they had Alex Meier in their ranks, the forward who would later sign for Eintracht Frankfurt. 'Alex, you need to mark Mertesacker,' screamed their manager, Andy Bergmann. '*Mark him!*' It didn't help. The cross came in, both of us jumped, and I slammed the ball into the far corner, right under the bar. 3-3. Moments like that boosted my self-esteem immensely. I wasn't quite sure what exactly all this meant for my future. Truth be told, I didn't get any opportunity to think about it, because school was still happening at the same time. The objective hadn't changed: *Abitur* first, then university for a degree in sports. My father probably would've liked to see me follow in his footsteps at the bank, but it was my brother who ended up going down that road. He'd always been more the banking type. I never had definitive job plans. In the back of my mind, I was considering maybe taking up with teams like Neustadt, Wunstorf, Arminia Hannover, Hildesheim, or Havelse. Somewhere around Hannover, in the sixth division, or maybe even the fourth. It was where some of my former teammates from Hannover's academy were to be found, playing football and doing an apprenticeship with the sponsors or the owners' companies. This strategy would've been on the cards for me, too, but after everything I'd seen, I hardly dared dream of a professional contract. As far as I was concerned, it was enough to master the challenges of everyday life. It was great just riding the wave, and I wanted to stick at it.

After tenth grade, I switched schools. Carl Friedrich Gauß sixth form college in Hemmingen, just north of Pattensen, was Hannover's partner school. Their PE teacher was our Under-19s manager, Joachim Hofmann, who lead the sports tutoring project, which involved extra lessons for swimmers, rowers, tennis players, wrestlers, and footballers. The situation was very convenient for me: training was scheduled early, which meant you could catch up on missed lessons in the afternoon. Granted, the system didn't apply during sixth form, but from time to time (and with the school's permission) I still attended training and caught up with the coursework on my own. Back then, we trained three or four times a week, much less than is common with today's youth. The real training, though, the real skill required came in the form of things outside of football: self-discipline and organisation. No one was there to tell me what to take with me the next day, where to go, or what to do. I had to think of everything in advance. Some days looked like this: early training, lessons, regular training with Hannover, and homework or studying in between. I'd be hauling three bags onto the bus. It's how you learned to deal with certain things, how to solve the smaller problems. Later, I realised how much my passing those little tests early on had helped me. As a result, I was better prepared whenever things on the pitch took a stressful turn.

For me, it was important to maintain a balance. On the one hand, you had the demands of competitive sport and the associated limits, which are really quite narrow. When my friends were doing weed, I'd be by the window, gasping for fresh air. I didn't want anything to do with it. It made my eyes burn — that couldn't be good, could it? — and I worried about my lungs. 'Someone open a window!' I'd shout. Every now and then, I was mocked and called a bore for my attitude, while they were sitting on the sofa smoking their rubbish and complaining about the cold. It would've been easier just to join in, but I had to decide what was more important. I was very aware of the fact that I was making a choice. At the time, there was also a small right-wing movement in Pattensen. A few boys would meet up to listen to Böhse Onkelz and trade ideas about that sort of thing. I went to check it out once but found I wasn't pulled in. It just wasn't on. 'I've got training, sorry.' Football saved me from drifting off in the wrong direction. I preferred watching Hannover play in the third division and listening to the drummers in the stands.

It was the communal experience that meant something to me, and it was really what moved me at that age. I still wanted to play as much a part in local life as possible. I didn't want to lose the feeling of being an ordinary boy from the neighbourhood, who could sometimes get up to no good. Any encounters with alcohol were usually based on dares – wheat beer mixed with cola or banana flavouring were the most frequent combinations. The ambition was to be cool, to show the others how tough you were, how much you could stomach. Alcohol poisoning and hospital admissions weren't uncommon, but for me, thank God, things stayed the right side of the line. When the opportunity arose, you'd brave the diving board at the public pool with a dozen shots of *Lüttje Lage* inside you: draft beer mixed with Korn schnapps, a Hannoverian specialty. But only if there was no game scheduled in the near future.

At school, many respected my need to deal with certain things in a different way. Others sneered at me: they probably thought me square. Playing for Hannover might have made me more popular with the girls, but I didn't really notice that. I had a girl-friend and I was never the sort to jump from one girl to the next. In any case, I was late to the whole kissing and sex thing and took my time instead. Really, I wasn't very cool. If any girls did fancy me, I didn't notice. I didn't want to be treated like someone special just because I could kick a ball around. My friends, for instance, knew I was normal and made sure I stayed grounded. I didn't feel special, either. My parents taught me to stay true to myself and to respect others, to treat them like I wanted them to treat me. It should've been the world's simplest concept, but it kept surprising people who didn't know me well.

One of those moments occurred during a school trip in year eleven. The whole year, all four classes, went to Poland, where we visited the Auschwitz memorial and museum. It was an incredible experience: the horrors that had happened there were unimaginable and the silence numbed our senses. None of us could speak; cold sweat was running down my back. The whole year was in tears. Eventually, it became too much for one boy. He was looking at pictures of murdered children on a wall behind thousands of shoes and suitcases when he finally broke down. 'Come,' I said, and put my arm around him. On the way back, he approached me to say thank you and to tell me how he wouldn't have thought I was the type for such a gesture. 'You're at 96, and you'll go pro soon,' he said, bewildered. 'How could you put your arm around me? You don't even know me.' For me, it was an interesting insight into peoples' reactions to celebrity. Or, in my case, *perceived* celebrity: from a distance, they put you onto an imaginary pedestal, which leads them to think you're looking down on them. After a while, I think, even the boys from that Hemmingen school who didn't know me at all understood that I wasn't like that.

I remained in the starting line-up during my second year with the Under-19s, too. The team was good: we had a genuine shot at winning the league. Ralf Rangnick and Mirko Slomka, Hannover's Bundesliga managers, were watching our games frequently. After I hadn't heard from the Lower Saxon FA for five years, I was called up to the Under-20s squad: they needed a centre-half. As I heard later on, Jürgen Stoffregen had called a colleague at the association with a recommendation.

'Listen, you've got so many flops on that team, just go and take that Mertesacker kid with you,' is how I imagine the conversation went. These boys were born in 1983, which meant I was by far the youngest. It was the first time I'd been among older players, but I coped quite well. When we reached the final of a regional Under-20s cup competition, we were watched by Matthias Sammer's father, who at the time was scouting for the German FA. Unfortunately, his presence didn't lead to an invitation to one of their courses.

In 2003, we were runners-up in the league, and qualified for the quarter-finals of the German Under-19s championship. We lost the first leg 0-1 to 1860 in Munich. The weather during the second leg was brutally hot, and I had a terrible day in front of Rangnick and Slomka. For a long while, we were 2-0 up but thanks to me we conceded two minutes before the final whistle, and the game went to extra time and penalties. As captain, I took responsibility for my mistake and, of course, missed my penalty. Out we went. My father was annoyed, and I was annoyed with him because he didn't console me, but on that day he simply wasn't up to it. He was too cross: being head of youth at Hannover made him responsible, which made this *his* defeat too — and one brought on by his own son, no less. Somehow, though, despite my poor performance in Munich, Rangnick invited me along to the first team's camp in Austria. I was well on the way. Finally.

People like to blame their problems on external factors or the harmful influence of others. Conversely, many are adamant that their success is largely based on their own skill and effort. Too quickly, they forget the crucial roles played by their social environment, their upbringing, and other privileges millions of people can't even imagine. Not everyone grows up in a sheltered family home, in an affluent country like Germany, with a father who invests his every minute in football, and a mother who is unconditionally supportive. Not everyone can attend school for thirteen years and try, on the side, to turn their hobby into a career. Not everyone ends up being a footballer, head of a company (like my brother Timo), or a tradesperson (my brother Denis). Not everyone grows up surrounded by local pitches and pools. I'm aware that I've been incredibly lucky in that respect.

Thanks to its great location, our little town has grown a lot over the recent years. Five new residential areas have been added, and students wanting to do their *Abitur* at my old school are — hopefully — no longer outsiders, because the school now offers the qualification. Because Denis and my parents still live there, Pattensen is still my home and my main port of call in Germany. I know exactly where I come from and how much I owe the people there, which is why it's very important to me to be involved locally.

Under my brother Timo's direction, the Per Mertesacker Foundation works to support TSV Pattensen, educational institutions, and the integration of children in the region. It's an awful lot of fun to achieve concrete aims alongside people who advocate the concerns of others with an enormous amount of enthusiasm. Co-financing a new stand, providing boots for refugee children, or introducing underprivileged kids to football.

For me, this all comes with being a representative for both town and region. I'm glad to be able to show people I haven't forgotten my roots.

2

BUNDESLIGA

HANNOVER 96

MY FIRST TRAINING CAMP WITH THE SENIORS WAS held in Austria, in July 2003. I was eighteen, about to start my final year at school, and didn't know if I was coming or going. Manager Ralf Rangnick had invited me and Under-23s teammate Björn Lindemann to pre-season training. We were both born in 1984, but Björn had played for the Under-19s for two or three years before me. He was one of those players who, not long before, had seemed on a completely unobtainable level to me. A huge talent, he was a playmaker with an eye for goal and a ruthless left foot.

During training, I couldn't keep up. I felt so overwhelmed that some situations left me in a daze. If I made mistakes during possession practice, players would scream at me at close range and at deafening volume. A 'What is this shit?' or even a 'Fucking hell!' would ring out across the pitch. Rangnick, who had a teaching degree in English, had introduced some, well, *technical* terms from the UK into the vernacular. Playing alongside people with Bundesliga experience threw me off course; training swept over me like a big wave. I was convinced things weren't going to work out.

The most technically gifted in the squad was Jan Šimák, a Czech. I had no way of defending successfully against him: his pace and precision with the ball drove me mad. While you could see his step-overs, turns, and feinted shots coming, you couldn't react to them. He pulled the rug from under your feet with his box of tricks; while you were still stumbling around in the dark, he'd already wafted away. Tragically (and ironically), his colossal talent ended up overexerting even himself: he couldn't cope with the demands of professional football and eventually just left Hannover. For weeks, he was nowhere to be found, apparently lost in depressive phases. After just six games during the 2003/04 season, he didn't return and signed with Sparta Prague the summer after.

Ralf Rangnick's (less-than-flattering) nickname was, and still is, 'professor', thanks to a TV interview he gave years ago in which, according to some traditionalists, his references to the advantages of the back four were overly intellectual. But he was an outstanding teacher who was constantly communicating with his players, especially the young ones. Many managers distance themselves from young players and, if anything, cultivate an air of aloofness. But Rangnick wanted to pass on his specialist knowledge. The majority of exercises he made us do — a back four with zonal defence and a high-press, co-ordinated runs in the attack — were still a novelty in Germany at the time. Rangnick was interested in me. He didn't leave me to struggle with the difficulties I had while settling in but corrected my mistakes with patience. He was impressed by my eagerness and my thirst for knowledge. His assistant Mirko Slomka, whom I knew from my time with the youth teams, also supported me in whatever way he could. Rangnick eventually gave me my big chance — just how great it was I only realised in hindsight. Fortunately, at the time, I wasn't burdened by pressure. I just wanted to play and had no idea that those weeks in Austria were setting the course for my future: one big blunder during training or one of the practice matches and I might have ended up back with the Under-23s — and who knows where that might have lead.

I made my unexpected debut for the first team during the Alpen Cup, a pre-season tournament. Back four regulars Vinicius Bergantin and Kostas Konstantinidis were sidelined with injuries for the game against Basel, and during the game, centre-half Dariusz Żuraw pulled a hamstring with a sliding tackle half an hour before the final whistle. Rangnick called me off the bench. 'Play the way you did with the Under-19s,' he said before sending me on my way. While we ended up losing on penalties, I was solid enough. That day, 7 July, happened to be Denis's birthday, and he was watching the match with Dad and Timo at Café Anno back in Pattensen. Two days later, I was on the pitch again for the third-place play-off against Dinamo Zagreb. They had Ivica Olić in their ranks, who would later play for Hamburg and Bayern.

I played another decent game, and for the first time ever, reporters surrounded me to ask how it felt, what I thought my prospects were, and so on and so forth. I wasn't prepared at all for this media onrush: never before had a journalist asked me my opinion, and what was more, no one from the club had taken me aside to explain how these question-and-answer games were played. Whatever you do, don't say the wrong thing and make headlines, I thought. Better to keep everything modest and un-spectacular. So I stood there, chatting cluelessly to these journalists without knowing what all of this actually meant, until eventually, our second 'keeper, Gerhard Tremmel, came round the corner and said, 'Just let the boy be already. He's only just played his second game.' It was a world without social media, and football wasn't all-consuming yet, either. Yes, I did follow the match reports in the papers, but I could disappear off the radar during the week. That anonymity helped me focus on the essentials without losing track of the big picture. Based on my passable performances at the camp, Hannover eventually offered me a contract as a token professional. Back then, Bundesliga regulations provided that every club had to employ at least twelve Germans, which was a protectionist measure due to the fact that sixty percent of players in the top flight were foreign. In reality, some clubs evaded this inconvenient law by carrying amateur players as official professionals, which is exactly what happened to me.

I didn't have an agent yet, so my father accompanied me to the talks with team manager Carsten Linke, during which I sat at the table and nodded along. Two thousand euros a month was the established rate for token pros, but my father said, 'A thousand six hundred is enough. But you need to guarantee that he'll actually train with the first team. That's worth more than money.' I didn't say anything. In my opinion, a thousand euros net was a lot: very good pocket money for someone still in education and living at home. In hindsight, this financially tame first step was a good experience for me. Imagine if we'd approached Hannover the way people do today, with our palms outstretched: 'Well, what can you provide for my son?' No. It was clear to my father that the primary concern wasn't money but the opportunity to progress. He showed me what really mattered.

As a young man, I learned a lot from my parents, especially that money and value are two completely separate things. After three months, Hannover raised my wages to €2,000 because they thought I was doing quite well during training with the first team. As token pro, you were assigned a fixed shirt number, usually one in the thirties. By chance, though, kitman Mille Gorgas came across my birthdate one day and gave me the 29. Again, I owed this bit of privilege to my father: thanks to him, I knew Mille and the secretary, Thomas Westphal, well and, as a result, was welcomed much more warmly than most youth players would've been. Mille liked to take me and Denis Wolf, one of my best mates from the Under-23s who was now training with the pros too, out to eat after training: chicken fried rice at Mr Phung's in the station concourse.

While I felt a part of Hannover's community, the climate in the dressing room was cold rather than welcoming. The older players couldn't care less if the new guy was homegrown. On the contrary, they considered you a rival from day one, someone who wanted to challenge them for their spot on the team. They snubbed you; sometimes, it bordered on bullying: Kostas Konstantinidis had his place opposite mine and would snap, 'What? What are you looking at? What do you want?' In his mind, my performances at the Alpen Cup were no longer relevant now that we were back in Hannover, and in any case, he was back on his feet now, so it was time for me to get lost.

Today, I get on splendidly with Kostas. In 2017, he was part of the charity match hosted in support of my foundation. We like to remember the old days. He was a merry guy, he'd really just been pulling my leg. But I didn't know that at the time. For me, it was pure psychological terror: I sat there, pigeon-chested, in a tiny dressing room amidst these hardened thirty-somethings, thinking, 'Please leave me alone, I don't mean anyone any harm!' I was seeking shelter and protection with the two or three other teenagers who were training at the top. We were all in the same boat. Denis was present a lot of the time, which was immensely important to me. He was a friendly face, someone who didn't want to drive me away. It doesn't compare to the present day, where newcomers are welcomed dutifully by the captain and immediately integrated as well as possible. The aim is to be a collective, a union, and as pleasant as that is, I'm still glad that my experience was different. I wouldn't hurt a fly back then, but in the end, I benefitted from having to prove myself on the pitch and being pestered in the dressing room by those who I wanted to replace. Suffering vengeful sliding tackles was part of everyday life, as was the discovery of Deep Heat in your pants. The latter, if you'll pardon the expression, burned your balls off. But you gritted your teeth and got on with it: it was clear that keeping your cool and demonstrating toughness was the only way to avoid any future bullying.

Training also demanded courage, if purely on a skill-based level. I remember a ricocheted shot I hammered into the upper corner with a perfect half-volley, cheered on by the handful of fans watching the session that day. That's how you earned your teammates' respect, but training well wasn't enough to be taken seriously by the established players. They kept a wary eye on your manner away from the pitch, too. It wasn't just about your skills as a player, you also had to respect the hierarchies and apply yourself to the best of your abilities. I wanted to show that I was someone who understood everything and on whom the group could rely: by lugging all sorts of items back and forth without complaining, for example. Goals, cones, bibs, and everything the kitman needed — youth players had to carry it all, not to mention pumping up the footballs. Everything had to be accurate. At away games, three or four of us, including Mille and the bus driver, would carry fifteen to twenty heavy iron crates from the bus to the dressing room and back. Even more rotten was lugging crates from the bus to the boot room on our return to Hannover late at night, when the older players had conveniently vanished. Because Hannover's ground was being rebuilt for the World Cup at the time, training turned into a long-distance trek. Temporary dressing rooms had been erected in the stadium gym, so taking the crates back and forth between there and the laundry room took absolutely ages. I was delighted whenever we were joined by two or three younger players who could lift heavy loads.

Admittedly, it certainly wasn't the most useful way to engage apprentice players, but it served an important purpose. As a young player, you learned to go about your day with your eyes wide open, to be alert, to watch out for anything to do, any tasks that needed fulfilling. For me, it wasn't a major adjustment: I'd been raised that way. In England, there used to be a decades-old tradition that decreed youth players had to clean the boots of the senior players. Today, that's no longer allowed. Youth players mustn't carry goals around anymore; it's against health and safety regulations. At most, they'll carry their designer wash bags. Everything's being arranged and sorted out for them. Doing something yourself or, God forbid, taking responsibility, has been abolished. I imagine this kind of full-time care doesn't do much to promote character development.

Before the 2003/04 winter break, I still played a few matches for the Under-23s but was taking part in most first-team training sessions and had started making the bench for games. Hannover had three centre-halves, so I was unofficially number four. Meanwhile, at school, trouble was on the horizon. Not all teachers showed the same understanding for my unusual situation. There were those who supported me by allowing me to bunk off a lesson or two when training got in the way. I was guaranteed full points in PE anyway, so my absence wasn't going to take away from that. Others, however, couldn't care less about my first attempts at walking among the first team. 'That's fine, I'll just award you zero points if you're not in class,' they'd say. As a sports tutor, Under-19s coach Joachim Hofmann was in regular contact with my teachers and tried to help me from the sidelines wherever he could.

For a long time, I resisted mobile phones. They were for self-important people, and, besides, it was always nice to have one or two hours to yourself on the bus, unreachable to the outside world. Whenever I needed to phone home to ask if I had to attend training at short notice, I borrowed a mobile from a classmate. But eventually, the club demanded I be accessible at any time. Training times were scheduled and changed spontaneously; sometimes, I was added to the squad on match day because one of the regulars had been sidelined. Whether I liked it or not, I had to jump on the mobile bandwagon.

It was paramount for Ralf Rangnick that I be successful at school and do my exams, to the extent that he called on the headmaster to ask politely that training and lessons be coordinated as smoothly as possible, so that I might combine both without major setbacks. I'll never forget his support. For me, it was a positive signal, a broad hint that he saw an actual chance for me. I wanted to take that chance in any way I could. In the first round of the DFB-Pokal – the German Cup – Rangnick brought me on for the first time. We had no problem keeping a clean sheet against fifth-division side VfL Kirchheim/Teck and ended up winning 3-0. From day three of the Bundesliga season, I was a constant in the squad but wasn't called into action. My lack of experience would've been a reason, but it wasn't only one.

I had allowed myself a pretty stupid indiscretion. One day, after a match, I'd stayed behind in the dressing room wing with Mille and Thommy Westphal, where Mille had invited me to have some food. Together, we scoffed a few kebabs. There wasn't a soul in sight until suddenly, a member of the coaching staff came through a door and noticed the dubious company. The next day, a meeting was scheduled. Rangnick called for more discipline in front of the whole team and ordered me to his office afterwards. At first, I had no idea what he wanted. 'If you get up to this kind of nonsense again, you're dead meat,' he bellowed. I was terribly embarrassed.

To get to the game against Eintracht Braunschweig at the end of October, I had to follow the team by car because school finished late. It was an evening match, a derby, and the Braunschweig supporters were frothing at the mouth. Warming up behind the touchline, I was surprised by the hatred that met me. It's not like anyone knew who I was. They didn't spit on me, but the noise was deafening. Although I wasn't technically on the pitch, it was an extreme experience: it helped me understand that if you wanted to play at this level, you didn't only have to beat the opponent but all of your personal insecurities too. You can't simply play a calm pass when an entire ground wants to eat you alive; you have to learn to tune out the hostility. In the end, I didn't play and we lost 2-0 — a disgrace, seeing as Braunschweig, our great rivals, were only in the third division back then. Westphal bawled his eyes out while the Braunschweig fans celebrated loudly and aggressively around our bus. To us, it was the end of the world.

The next day, many Hannover supporters arrived at the club's premises to vent their spleen. Training happened under siege; it was like being in a pressure cooker. Rangnick's reputation was in trouble after the debacle. He wanted to teach one or two starting players a lesson, and so replaced half the team for the Bundesliga game against Cologne. On top of that, right-back Steven Cherundolo had suffered a hamstring injury. Because Rangnick wanted us to be stable at the back, he let me play Cherundolo's position during final training. To my surprise, I was part of the starting XI. The evening before the match, I approached our masseuse at the team hotel. 'I'll be playing tomorrow; I need a massage, please,' I said. 'Okay,' came the reply, 'but you'll have to wait until everyone else is done.' My turn didn't come until 11pm, but I was still excited. This was a real accomplishment: young players weren't usually considered for a massage; it wasn't even open for debate. A request was typically followed by a snippy rejection: 'We're full.' Waiting on the actual massage bench sent the wrong signal to older players, masseuses, therapists, and coaches. Professional football isn't just a matter of performance but of physical robustness and the ability to withstand suffering, too. Youth players were neither allowed nor encouraged to show any signs of weakness, and entering the seniors' medical unit was generally frowned upon.

The first time I was offered physio was when I was with the Under-19s. After training, two therapists tended to the players, but you often had to wait your turn patiently for two or three hours. Here, too, older players came first. Because Joachim Hofmann lived in the neighbouring village and so was able to give me lifts home, I would wait a long time and was finally on the receiving end of a treatment or two. The physios would use pens to draw lines on my back, which were supposed to improve my posture. I didn't understand what exactly they were doing but accepted it nonetheless. You weren't given massages, though. I got a reality check when I joined the national team a year later. I realised there were major differences between physiotherapists and massage therapists. The *DFB* doesn't just host the best players but the best carers, too. It's where I met Klaus Eder and Dr Hans-Wilhelm Müller-Wohlfahrt, who would both come to treat me for a long time. The feeling of being advised in a competent manner is absolutely crucial for sportspeople.

I was terribly lucky that Eder was interested in me. I think he considered me a challenge: he'd never before got his hands on such a lanky beanpole. At our first meeting, Klaus stood before me, slightly crooked. He wanted to show me how poor my running posture was. If not corrected and compensated, this could have vast ramifications for my limbs and lead to immense problems. I realised that Klaus was of such quality both as a therapist and as a person that he had the power to influence my career. He knew which pressure points to touch and which vertebrae to set, which isn't something you could say of every physio. We got along instantly. His care helped me survive the next training session or enabled me to play after having been injured. It made me realise how vital those treatments were. People underestimate the physical and psychological strain involved in professional football, especially for young players who'd only just outgrown puberty.

In any case, with the guaranteed spot at the back against Cologne, I was officially entitled to my first massage. I was still last, but even so. When I returned to our room at eleven, Kostas was already asleep. When we finally played Cologne, our own fans took revenge for our inexcusable failure against Braunschweig. We were outplayed, and yet, without any discernible possession, we suddenly took the lead through Thomas Brdarič, before Matthias Scherz got the equaliser before the break. We were getting off lightly. I struggled during the first half and had to be substituted in the second. The long march to the dressing rooms — Cologne's ground was also being remodelled for the World Cup — was an awful experience. According to Daniel Stendel, my teammate at the time, I huffed and puffed my way up the tunnel, groaning that it was over for me. I was completely exhausted. 'I can't go on,' I stammered at Mirko Slomka in the showers. I was replaced by a heavily-bandaged Cherundolo, and we even managed to turn the match around, with Stendel making it 2-1. Apparently, I hadn't been prepared after all. At least not to play right-back, a position that I'd never played before, not least to Bundesliga standard. I wasn't made for running up and down the line. I wasn't up to the challenge, neither physically nor psychologically. In the end, the acid test tore me apart: *Kicker* magazine slapped me with a 5. *Kicker*'s ratings follow German school grades: 1 is very good, 6 is considered inadequate. Not a good start.

After my dismal debut, I didn't play in a single game for four months; I fell off the map for a while. During the winter, we signed five new players, including Abel Xavier, a colourful Portuguese madman. He wore red Puma boots with his blond mohawk and was constantly surrounded by beautiful women. Once during training, he left the warm-up, jumped the hoardings, and threatened to beat up a *Bild* journalist about a less-than-flattering story. All the while, the rest of the team continued to run their laps, and eventually, Xavier rejoined them as if nothing had happened.

For resident nippers Denis and me, Daniel Stendel was crucial to our integration, mainly because he allowed us to sit at the poker table on the team bus. As a young player, the bus initially makes you very uncomfortable. While you're trying to find your seat, older players will dismissively wave you away from theirs: 'Get lost, this is where I'm sitting.' Luckily, there were two empty seats at Daniel and Silvio Schröter's little table, but obviously, there was a price to pay for our shelter. We were skinned during game after game of thirty-one. The stakes were only a few pfennigs – equal to one hundredth of a mark – high, but Daniel was even more competitive at the poker table than on the pitch. For him, it was a matter of prestige. The goal was to outdo the others and fluster them so they made mistakes and were thrown off even more. Style was imperative, too: stay cool, keep your head, and with a bit of luck, the game was yours. Daniel couldn't deal with being beaten, but when he snapped, it was best to ignore him rather than hit back. The right blend of courage and humility was important: he was allowed to lose his cool, we weren't — as a seasoned professional, he was exempt from the rules that applied to us. Still, it was invaluable for us to be in steady contact with two regulars. We were glad to pay our three euros per trip if it meant we were part of something greater.

Eleven matchdays before the end of the season, Rangnick ordered me back into the starting line-up for an away game in Gladbach. I gave a decent performance, and *Kicker* gave me a 4 this time – adequate. We lost 1-0, though, and found ourselves fifteenth in the table, a single point above the relegation zone. Rangnick and Slomka were fired. Rangnick said goodbye the following day with a rather emotional speech that brought tears to the eyes of some in the squad. Along with sympathy for a very good coach, we had feelings of guilt — after all, we were the reason he'd lost his job. For me personally, though, the managerial change was a blessing. Ewald Lienen backed me from day one: 'I'll have the beanpole play!' It was unusual to entrust a key position in the centre of defence to such an inexperienced player. But according to Lienen, during his time in Spain, 'no one cared about age, including me'. From that moment on, I played next to Vinicius. Kostas, who'd been a constant under Rangnick, was dropped to the bench.

Lienen's reputation was that of a brusque, humourless oddball obsessed with nutrition and exercise. They call him Zettel-Ewald – zettel translates as note in English – because he was constantly writing things down on the bench. Discipline, particularly during training, was especially important to him; you always had to give it your all and show the right attitude. He turned out to be a completely different kind of manager. After dinner on the night before games, he'd tell outrageous stories during team meetings, taking the mickey out of the press, his players, and himself. With relish in his voice, he'd make fun out of journalists while at the same time lifting the mood in the room. 'Just imagine,' he'd say, 'when those hacks get old, their faces will be wrinkled and decayed because of all their negativity.' He'd paint flowery pictures of Jiří 'Staini' Štajner pelting down some country road to his home in the Czech Republic. During his recitals, Lienen would sweat so badly, he had to pat himself down with a hand towel. The squad would sit around him in a horseshoe, crying tears of laughter. Occasionally, his assistant Michael Frontzeck, a bone-dry, seasoned man, had to rope him back in on nights like this: 'Ewald, that's enough now.' The two of them made a perfect pair.

Our first game under the new leadership was a defeat to Kaiserslautern, causing us to slip into the relegation zone. At least it wasn't my fault. On the contrary, I'd played my best game to date: a 3 on the *Kicker* scale. Two days later, however, I was admitted to Frederikenstift hospital to have my nose bent back into shaped after Marijan Christow had shattered it three minutes before the final whistle. I was pretty groggy straight after surgery, but once the anaesthesia had worn off five hours later, I wanted to leave the hospital at once. The next day, I was fitted for a mask by a specialist in orthopaedics so I could rejoin training. Breathing through it was a struggle; I was sweating like a pig, and my peripheral vision had gone completely. Back then, these masks weren't yet light plexiglas but chunky black monsters. Presumably, Ewald wouldn't have held it against me if I'd cried off for the Schalke game, but that was out of the question. I neither could nor wanted to skirt the challenge. I can probably trace this attitude back to my parents' home: Mum and Dad taught me not to lose my head over complications, and that problems were just simple facts that had to be overcome

In Gelsenkirchen, I encountered Ebbe Sand for the first time. The Dane was a master of movement; it was extremely difficult to anticipate his runs. He'd approach, drop off, feint again, play a short pass, then all of a sudden a long one: it was impossible to keep up with him. In the back four, you didn't need to focus on a single player and were able to solve many situations with team-work, but my restricted vision made it difficult. Sand got me so fidgety that I ended up putting through my own net to make it 1-1. He would've scored anyway, but still — my first own goal. We took the lead again, only for Sand to equalise late on. *Kicker* score: 4. These were negative experiences that I couldn't allow to break me.

'Don't lose heart,' said Lienen. 'The next game's coming up.' He'd address my mistakes openly but never hold them against me: he wanted me to learn, that was the priority. Next up was a home match against Dortmund, who had massive Jan Koller in attack (1-1, *Kicker* score: 3) and then a 2-0 win over 1860 Munich (*Kicker* score: 4). We were out of the relegation woods. The mix of maximum focus on the pitch and necessary ease off it, brought into the squad by Lienen, was what made the difference: a team that had been so disjointed all year was suddenly functioning. Even though Lienen didn't say much to me in general, he always gave me the feeling he had a high opinion of me. 'Nice work, beanpole!' he'd shout during coordination exercises, 'Well done!' He also approved greatly of the fact that I already had a girlfriend. 'You're spoken for? Very good. Bang on. You go ahead, do your thing.' I think he felt we could do without party animals and bullshitters in the fight for survival. He didn't like people who were out all night at all.

Ewald was the kind of manager who wanted to see a healthy dose of toughness on the pitch. We were supposed to take care not to provoke any unnecessary bookings or free-kicks but were still allowed to show others who was boss. The game in general, however, was on the brink of change. Defenders were no longer given the first foul free of charge and tackling from behind was now outlawed. Anyway, apart from this process of civilisation on the pitch, I wasn't the type of defender to put down markers or to try and intimidate forwards physically. It didn't fit my character, and in any case, I was a lousy actor: no one would've bought my pantomime hard man routine. My aim was always to find fair solutions; it was an approach with which I could identify. The calculation was simple: fewer fouls meant fewer set-pieces against us.

Old-school defenders like Jürgen Kohler and Thomas Berthold, who'd been real man-to-man markers, were often quite negative about me in public. They would've preferred to see me rushing into a tackle and knocking someone out. We were built differently. Coaches and teammates were glad that someone was playing a neat ball without giving up possession. My speciality was keeping my distance and evaluating the situation before stealing the ball at the last moment. Opposition players were shocked at how good my feet were and that a beanpole like me could play on the floor. Ewald especially valued my pragmatic approach to the game. I never had the feeling I had to do anything special or something extra; he was after efficiency more than anything else. I followed the same routine as I did with the Under-17s: feign returning the ball to the 'keeper, then turn and pass to the deep-lying midfielder. Those were my tactics, the ones I knew I'd mastered. Sidesteps were also part of my repertoire, but they were less than popular with Ewald. 'Do that again and you're out,' he threatened.

These days, the requirements for my position have changed. Centre-halves on the better teams need to be playmakers in disguise. The sixty-yard diagonals that defenders like Jérôme Boateng manage to play without thinking didn't exist in my early days. During my first five Bundesliga years, I probably didn't play a single risky pass into midfield; I'd go round the back or lay off to my nearest teammate. Struggling against relegation in my very first season wasn't ideal. Luckily, though, I had no real overview of the pressure weighing on the club. I was free as a bird; I didn't know what was really going on. I don't remember when it started, but there were a dozen times when diarrhoea forced me onto the toilet before matches and when I regularly felt nauseous before kick-off, with blood shooting to my eyes. I'd turn my head to one side so my teammates wouldn't notice. Because I stopped eating four hours before games, I never actually vomited — occasionally some tomato soup — but the urge to relieve myself and throw up before kick-off never completely went away. For me, it was part of the game; I thought it was normal. It's only now, after my career has ended, that I realise how much strain my body was under, week in and week out. The nausea was part of a fight-or-flight response: stress hormones released in the brain signal to the stomach to get rid of any food residue as fast as possible, because all the blood and energy used for digestion is now urgently required somewhere else. In your legs, for example. It's mad how much of an effect football has on a person without them realising. Professional sports force you to switch off these psychosomatic strains like a TV programme you don't want to watch. But, of course, it keeps running. Quietly, in the background.

The season's busy phase coincided with my *Abitur* exams. I was rushing from appointment to appointment without time to think. From Monday to Friday, when I was sitting next to my classmates, fighting for good grades, all the exciting stuff — the glittering Bundesliga snow globe, massive crowds, crucial matches everywhere — was further away than Paris from Pattensen. And it was better that way. I managed to remain relatively calm, because I was sure I'd make it. It wasn't going to be the best exam ever sat but it was an exam nonetheless. In early May, I took the four-hour-long maths exam followed by final training and then a relegation play-off against Eintracht Frankfurt. It was stressful, but I coped. We ended up winning 3-0, saving ourselves from relegation, and I managed to bag an *Abitur* score of 2.8. During the Leavers' Ball, the results of a survey were read aloud: Who's got the best hair cut? Who wears the flashiest clothes? Who'll be a millionaire? Who's got the best car? I won the last two. Granted, it made sense: I was already driving a Mercedes A-Class, and though the wages and transfer fees weren't yet as grotesque as they are today, the idea that I might become established in professional football on long-term basis genuinely didn't appear far-fetched any more. I had been a regular in the second half of the season as we secured our place in the Bundesliga once more.

By the end of the month, I'd signed a new contract until 2008, giving me considerably higher earnings. It had been negotiated by my agent, Roman Pletz, who'd been recommended to me by Marc Ziegler. I was now officially a full-time professional, but I still didn't feel like one yet. At the start of the 2004/05 season, I was a nineteen-year-old rookie who'd just made his way through his first Bundesliga matches, when a goalkeeper named Robert Enke entered our dressing room and welcomed me. 'Ah, so you're Per.' He'd come from Spain, where he'd been playing for Barcelona. He was 27, and from the outset, made me feel like he valued me. Me, the newbie. I was the defender, he was the 'keeper: he had my back in every sense of the word. He encouraged me, told me I'd be making my way, and made me aware of my qualities — qualities that my insecurities at times wouldn't let me see. He was placing his trust in me, and I don't think there's a better feeling to have at work, no matter your profession. As a young defender, it was crucial to my development. The thought that I didn't need to be afraid if I didn't clear a cross was invaluable: I knew Robert would be there. He had an aura of calm and determination. In football, we describe him as a leader. Very few teammates had such a positive effect on me and my career.

Ewald Lienen's decision to use me in the defence was encouraging, too. During the second league game in Dortmund, I asserted myself after a corner against Jan Koller in a duel of giants, scoring the equaliser in the last minute with a header. My first Bundesliga goal. A month later, I was spending my birthday with my girlfriend, when the phone rang. Unknown number. I expected a well-wisher but recognised the voice on the other end at once: Jürgen Klinsmann, national team manager. He wasn't aware it was my birthday and instead told me that he was adding me to the squad for the upcoming Iran friendly. "We want to introduce a breath of fresh air into the team," was vaguely how he expressed it. 'I'm bringing in new players now, a new generation. Lahm, Podolski, Schweinsteiger, Hitzlsperger, Huth.' I don't remember saying much, other than, 'Yeah, cool, thanks.' I was completely blindsided by the whole thing. For a few seconds, I was enjoying an outer-body experience, watching myself having a phone conversation with the national team manager. Or rather, him having one with me; the national team hadn't been on my radar in the slightest. When Klinsmann finally hung up, I felt like I'd grown another five centimetres.

I couldn't stay on cloud nine for long, though. In Germany, males either had to do military service or service in the civil protection until conscription was put into abeyance by the government on 1 July 2011. The day after my call-up, it was back to my alternative civilian service in an institution for the mentally ill. Preparing their meals, making their beds, taking them to the toilet; that was my job for three to four hours a day. My older brother had joined the army and enjoyed it. As a top athlete, you could expect various mitigations and coordinate your training schedule to suit you, so I did genuinely consider copying him, but my gut said no. *You're not doing that; you're claiming conscientious objection.* I wanted to help people, not be on duty clutching a weapon. But that aside, I didn't want things handed to me, either. Having my life made easier because I was a footballer wasn't for me. It would've embarrassed me terribly in front of my friends, who had to take the normal route after school. My conscience wouldn't have coped with being given preferential treatment.

During my final year in school, I'd had to turn down the study tour to Florence due to my development at Hannover. That hadn't come easy to me, especially following the moving experiences in Poland two year before. I didn't want special treatment. Yes, I was playing Bundesliga football for Hannover at weekends, but afterwards, I was quick to return to my boys in Pattensen and come back down to Earth. That's how I wanted to be perceived, not like some puffed-up popinjay who thought he was something special because he could kick a ball around. There were templates for conscientious objection on the internet. With my mother's help, I found the appropriate form ('The use of firearms is contrary to my basic convictions', etc.) and sent it off. It was approved, but I still had to be present for inspection. My degree of fitness was T2, only second best because of my height. 'You're too tall for a tank or submarine,' the physician explained with a straight face. Hannes Winzer and Denis Wolf, two friends from the Under-19s, suggested I try the Wahrendorff clinic in Ilten, between Hannover and Pattensen. They had both done their service there and said it had been a good experience.

The clinic was willing to cooperate with 96; I called on the club and was granted the placement. 'The closed ward is best for you,' they told me at the clinic. 'You'll get a key and will be able to make up your own schedule after training. You can come and go without hassle.' There were fifteen patients in my department, all between thirty and fifty years old, who were cared for around the clock — feeding, sleeping, changing, undressing. Some had manic depression, some were severely autistic, others would lie on their beds in a vegetative state for 23 hours a day, staring at the wall and only leaving their rooms at meal times. The psychological conditions and symptoms varied. Some could speak, some couldn't. One patient was a competent chess player and told me about everything under the sun, another ran at me and yanked a meal tray from my grasp. You never really knew what could happen. One person, a single man, knew who I was. His name was Manni. Manni liked to watch TV, but more than that, he loved to read car magazines. He could recite every piece of equipment by heart and knew which model had electric windows and which had a satnav. Manni was also allowed to leave the ward for a few minutes every now and then. I'd accompany him to the canteen for a bratwurst. The minute I stepped into the corridor, he'd rush up to me and smothered me with kisses. None of the patients were violent — you didn't need to protect yourself from them — but nonetheless, there was a reason the ward was closed in the way you'd imagine: plexiglas, heavy doors, and so forth. These men weren't capable of surviving in the outside world.

Processing those experiences day after day wasn't easy, because I had never dealt with mentally ill people before. In our society, the subject is almost taboo; these people aren't seen or heard. The ten months spent in their company broadened my horizons significantly. I felt great respect for the three or four permanent carers, who were lovingly looking after their patients; they were subjected to enormous amounts of psychological strain every day themselves and did it all for little pay. They were Hannover fans, all of them. The club was their passion, the thing they clung to when their work got tough. For me, the contrast couldn't be greater. One moment, you were training, signing autographs, and playing in front of 60,000 adoring fans; the next, you were on a closed ward with people who needed medicating and couldn't accomplish even the simplest tasks by themselves. Every day, Wahrendorff made me realise how lucky I was: I was able to help people who were entirely dependent on the support of others. It wasn't a chore, it was a gift. Without it, something would've been missing in my personal development. I might not have come as far I did, either as a person or as an athlete. I'm convinced that one is linked to the other. Many people aren't aware of their good fortune. As a young player in modern professional football, you're shielded from all negative things and thoughts, which quickly leads to a loss of awareness. In my opinion, the fact that young players in academies barely get to see anything but footballs is a huge problem. In the long run, without a change of perspective, it becomes almost impossible for a player to compartmentalise properly. As a result, even the slightest setback can seem like a crisis.

The mood at Hannover remained tense during the first months of the season. We were bottom of the league before the away game at Hansa Rostock. After the loss to newly-promoted Arminia Bielefeld at home, there were calls of 'Lienen out'; the local papers were negative towards him, too. Lienen had even fallen out with some of the players after criticising their body fat levels. He was on the verge of being replaced. The team saved his job, though, with a 3-1 win in Rostock. Two weeks later, during our 2-0 win over Borussia Mönchengladbach, I scored my second league goal, but Ilja Kaenzig, Hannover's director of football, was of the opinion that our collective and individual performances weren't being duly acknowledged by the public. 'If Per had played a game like that for Bayern Munich, the whole country would be celebrating him right now,' he said with a hint of bitterness in his voice. Still, at least *Kicker* gave me a 2.

We won five consecutive games and found ourselves unexpectedly on course for the UEFA Cup just before Christmas and ended the 2004/05 season in a decent tenth place. Yet Kaenzig, who had previously been Reiner Calmund's assistant at Leverkusen, was not entirely convinced by Lienen. It seemed he was merely waiting for the opportunity to replace him with his own choice, and after a few months of unsatisfying results the next season, that time came. Peter Neururer took the wheel. He was famous for talking big in public but always remaining more measured internally. 'I criticise the footballer, never the person,' he said frequently, a sentence that would burn itself into my mind.

Neururer had us practice the basics (set-pieces, build-up, etc.) and demanded I play simply at the back. In addition, by use of a little trick, he wanted to find out if there were any interpersonal issues in the team. We all had to write down the name of the person with whom we didn't want to share a room under any circumstances. My bunkmate at the time was Frankie Juric, the very relaxed, easy-going goalkeeper from Australia. He always stayed calm before games, which made him the perfect roommate. I wrote down Michael Delura. He was a nice guy but very young and boisterous. He had joined us on loan from Schalke under a shower of premature praise. While his technique was brilliant, he also had a girlfriend whom he called 'my little rocket' and who was putting stupid ideas in his head. I was afraid of being distracted, but I don't know how much Neururer found out about our individual issues in the end.

In my three seasons at Hannover, we fought relegation three times. A figure of speech in German football decrees that you must bite and scratch your way out of the bottom of the league, but in my opinion, clean and successful tackles were more valuable to the team. In 74 matches, I was only booked twice. Later, I collected a few red cards, but they were always due to professional fouls born out of desperation, in situations where you faced a clear choice: be sent off or concede. I never hurt an opponent on purpose; that wasn't my game, because it would've only done damage to the team and myself. It was more likely that was I was on the receiving end, like in the winter of 2005. With the ball out of play, Miroslav Klose lunged into a nasty tackle, catching me badly and tearing a couple of ligaments in my ankle joint. I had to leave the pitch before even an hour was played and was now facing my first-ever operation. To add insult to injury — quite literally — we ended up losing the match by 4-1.

Like almost every other international, I travelled to Munich for treatment with Müller-Wohlfahrt. He had Germany's best surgeons at his disposal and sent me to Klaus Eder's Donaustauf clinic for my rehab. The DFB specified this particular procedure, so it was inevitable that I slipped into the machinery, but the club approved the process, because they knew I was in good hands. In Donaustauf, I learned what it meant to come back from an injury and how much of an impact expert treatments have on the healing process. The goal, of course, was the World Cup. After rehab, Miro called to apologise. He hadn't realised the ball had gone out and he didn't hurt me on purpose. That was it. Issue over.

In retrospect, Bundesliga life was fairer than I had imagined. There were only a few players who tried to provoke a reaction by trash talking you. During one game, Carsten Jancker, who was with Kaiserslautern at the time, repeatedly screamed into my ear. 'Go on, then, go run to your boy Klinsi!' And while this is only the print friendly version, he didn't manage to faze me. The whole thing was so ludicrous, I couldn't help but laugh. I myself wasn't the type to chew off someone's ear or try to catch them out with some other psychological trick. No, my signature move was securing the ball correctly; dangerous sliding tackles weren't my style. The feeling of wanting to hurt someone presented itself only rarely, and I always managed to block it out again. As a rule, things got thorny whenever the Under-23s were summoned for practice matches. The boys were very enthusiastic, because they wanted to prove to their coaches and to themselves that they could take us on. We mostly just wanted to play at half speed, but if we didn't see much of the ball then, inevitably, there were clashes: some went full throttle, others broke out the dirty tackles. While this was common practice back then, inter-squad games are nearly always mixed now, preventing those situations before they can develop.

In the run-up to the World Cup, I was running the risk of getting into trouble with Granny Irmgard: Bayern had shown interest in me. I had to adhere to Roman Pletz's career plan, though, which dictated a targeted, step-by-step development. Many players had joined Bayern too early, and, as a result, had broken their stride because they hadn't been playing enough. Saying no to Uli Hoeneß couldn't have been easy for Roman, but he knew what was best for me. He also turned down an offer from Hamburg's sporting director, Didi Beiersdorfer. The next logical step was Werder Bremen: only a hundred kilometres from Hannover, always playing Champions League football, and a good stepping stone for young players.

The Bremen clique on the national team — Torsten Frings, Tim Borowski, Miroslav Klose — had already been badgering me on that front, raving about football life down by the Weser river. In the summer of 2006, I also faced a change in my private life. I had been with my girlfriend for just under three years, but the hustle and bustle around the World Cup at home had become too much for her; the spotlight and public attention just weren't her cup of tea. While I had tried to keep her out of the public eye, I hadn't always succeeded. When *Sport-Bild* magazine asked me how things were working out with my girlfriend, because I was still living in my parents' house in Pattensen, my answer was slightly offhand. 'We sleep in the basement; the walls are thick down there,' I said it without thinking. She didn't approve at all. Those were the first signs of trouble. During the tournament, she never wanted to sit in the VIP block with the other players' partners, because she knew that the papers were going to print the pictures the next day. It led *Bild* to wonder about the unfamiliar man sitting amidst the cluster of wives and girlfriends. The headline read 'Who is Mr X?' It was Mille. I had given him my girlfriend's VIP pass, because she preferred to sit unobserved in a regular block. Mille and I were so close that he accompanied me on every national team journey. During the *Sommermärchen*, he was Mister X. I liked that my girlfriend despised all this hype and fuss, because that's quite rare in football. Her thinking and mentality were so different from some of my teammates' partners, who enjoyed the interest and used it for their own gain. It was terribly important for me, especially during my first years as a professional: thanks to her — and my stable parental home — I didn't lose my head. I never had desire to savour the fame or felt the need to have amorous adventures in every town. Our relationship was much too valuable and much too strong. But, of course, I couldn't turn my back on football, couldn't exit from this stage. Eventually, all this became too much for her, and we parted amicably.

WERDER BREMEN

IN AUGUST 2006, THE TRANSFER TO BREMEN WAS complete. I was their record signing with a fee of €4.7 million plus a few extra clauses. We reached a contractual agreement that €50,000 of that fee be used to build an artificial pitch for Hannover's academy. It was a matter close to my heart, because I'd trained there with the boys on concrete and red cinder; the conditions for youth players weren't what they are today. Subsequently, Hannover president Martin Kind wrote me a letter of thanks, assuring me that he was going to follow my career. During my presentation in Bremen — I held up a green 29 shirt next to Klaus Allofs and Thomas Schaaf — press officer Tino Polster told me of the event's scale: 'N-TV are broadcasting this live; we've never had that happen before.'

The realisation that I had survived the World Cup at home was a great weight off my mind in July, but I still arrived at Werder while recovering from injury. After the semi-final defeat against Italy, I'd had surgery on my left heel. I'd been having issues since taking a knock there in February 2005. The bone had become deformed and was putting pressure on the Achilles tendon, which in turn resulted in chronic inflammation. I was just about able to cope with the pain during the tournament, but something still had to be done, and so with Werder's approval I returned to rehab with Klaus.

I wasn't spared my initiation at Werder, though. Things were a lot rougher than a bit of singing while standing on a chair in the dressing room. Everyone met in a bar in town that was reserved for the team, and every newbie had to have a drink with everyone who had been with the club for more than a year. On balance, that was 25 drinks, from cocktails to beer to vodka, which didn't end well. Every few minutes, another player would go to the bar and return with a tray of five drinks, one for them and four for the newbies: cheers, down in one. I was scared that my body would bloat badly, so I was armed with two huge bottles of still water, following each drink with half a litre to protect myself from the consequences of the hard liquor. It worked like a charm. Obviously, I went to the toilet about fifteen times, but somehow, I survived the evening. It turned into a boozy night, with everyone having to perform a song. I chose 'Er hat ein knallrotes Gummiboot', a song about a red boat, which didn't necessarily match Werder's colour scheme, but by then it didn't matter. Back at the hotel, I was completely shattered and couldn't tell up from down. I still had the sense to rest my injured left leg on a tower of cushions, though, to stop all the alcohol and water from collecting down there and opening the pores. The next morning, I woke up overjoyed: my foot hadn't swollen up. That night showed me the power of still water, which is why it's still my favourite drink to this day. But there were new signings who didn't get away as lightly as I had.

For my friend Mesut Özil, who joined us two years later, it turned into one of the worst nights of his life. He never forgot it. The subject came up a lot at Arsenal, and we couldn't help but laugh. He didn't know where he was and couldn't remember any details afterwards. All he knew was that he needed the toilet a lot and that sometimes, he didn't make it there in the first place. Nights like these brought us together as a team. Everyone wanted to get through initiation and earn themselves some respect at the bar. Granted, some managed this better than others.

Back then, my poison was a cocktail called 'vodka ahoj': vodka mixed with a raspberry candy fizz sold in Germany. Initially, they didn't serve it at *Modernes*, one of the best places in town, but for my sake, it was eventually introduced to the menu. It was very much a unique Mertesacker special. You should still be able to get it there today. I always carried a few packs of sherbet on me during those nights, just in case. At least vodka was relatively tolerable. In contrast, Naldo used to serve Stroh brand rum with an alcohol level of eighty percent: it took just one sip to intoxicate you. But we weren't boozing constantly; these dares only happened once a year. I don't know whether this tradition is still upheld in Bremen since the departure of Clemens Fritz as captain, but I hope so. You don't forget nights like this, full of song and laughter. They've given us the best stories, forever connected to sherbet.

The nice thing about Bremen were the different characters on the team. Both club and town were inherently reserved and, in true north German fashion, quite aloof, but it was uncomplicated and informal at the same time. The Weserstadion saw players from all corners of the earth come together, and with the exception of a few, everyone felt at ease. The cordiality was great, the distances short: it took ten minutes from my Schwachhausen home to the ground, ten from Schwachhausen to the airport, and ten from one end of town the other. Everyone knew everyone, and people were proud of their town and their club. While the localism was very pronounced, it was always accompanied by humour and humility.

There are few footballers who would say that their time in Bremen hasn't helped them. Even Serge Gnabry, who had arrived there from Arsenal, told me that it was one of the best decisions he had ever made. From a purely sporting point of view, leaving London for Bremen might initially be a step back. But sometimes, that step is merely preparation for a longer stride.

Serge says Bremen showed how important it is for a player to feel at ease in their environment and to really identify with a club, a town, and the associated values. If you don't develop any feeling for the shirt or for the people in the stadium, you won't get beyond a certain level. The feeling of applying yourself to something that's greater than your personal interests releases that extra ten or fifteen percent of performance that makes all the difference. That's the kind of motivation that genuinely counts; no money in the world offsets the joy of making people who mean a lot to you happy. Experiencing all this in Bremen helped Serge immensely, even though he only played there a year.

The Brazilian players especially showed how much of your form depends on your personal wellbeing. This correlation is completely underestimated by outsiders. Just like my fellow centre-back Vinicius when he was at Hannover, my defensive partner at Bremen, Naldo, performed at top level, because he coped well with northern climate and culture. Our forward, Diego, was technically advanced, a typical Brazilian on the ball, but at the same time he was astonishingly tough and resilient. He was able to focus entirely on football and, as a result, was a great success for the club. Others, however, pined for home, families, friends, sun, and native food. The defensive midfielder, Wesley, for example, who played for Werder from 2010 to 2012, wanted to get by in Bremen – he learned the language – but had difficulty adjusting. The attacking midfielder, Carlos Alberto, who joined Werder a year after me and inherited my title as record signing, had to sit down frequently during training in the winter months. He was broken by the weather. In Brazil, he had been magic: Thomas Schaaf told me how he had been an absolute hero during a cup game there, doing what he wanted, dribbling back and forth, taking liberties with everyone. In Germany, though, there was nothing of the sort. He failed the simplest manoeuvres; the ball wouldn't obey him. The frustration he felt because he couldn't be himself on the pitch made him lose his head: he brawled with teammates and bought beer from petrol stations late at night. All attempts to integrate him failed.

There were many extraordinary players in the squad: During his first few years, Baumi — Frank Baumann — was the kind of captain who controlled everything and gave off an air of authority. Torsten Frings, his successor as our defensive midfielder, was the great ringleader. He didn't beat around the bush and whenever necessary, put his foot down in the dressing room, too: 'Listen, men, this isn't right!' In time, I grew into a similar role, and while I didn't open my mouth immediately, as an international, I was shown respect from the start. People acknowledged my opinion. In training or during a match, everyone had to accept that I raised my voice every now and then to give commands or encourage teammates. On the pitch, you had to abandon any and all sensitivities and make success the priority. If someone screamed at you, it was for the greater good. Everything stayed outside, nothing was brought into the dressing room. In my eyes, Ivan Klasnić was one of our best forwards. He had that brilliant left foot and that trademark Croatian coolness in the box. He was obsessed with scoring goals, just like Claudio Pizarro, our insurance policy. Pizza was always relaxed, a real bon vivant, but you could always rely on him. Year after year, his South American cunning in the box and his phenomenal technique brought in the goals. Pizarro never raised his voice; instead, he helped many young players with his readiness to talk: he lent a sympathetic ear to them all. Everyone liked him, which is why he was welcomed back with open arms after his time at Bayern and Chelsea: we needed him.

On the surface our goalkeeper, Tim Wiese, with his pink shirt, was a misfit. He was a polarising character, but behind the scenes he was very quiet and disciplined: a professional through and through, yet funny and sociable at the same time. He was always good to have around. His goal was to be as athletic as possible, and he worked on his body with an incredible spirit in order to reach his ideal fighting weight. Nowadays, as a wrestler – he made his WWE debut in 2016 in Munich – this attitude hasn't changed. It's simply been applied to a different direction. We sat next to each other on the bus; it connected us. We were two completely different people, but somehow we spoke the same language. Tim was very superstitious and insisted we repeat certain sequences on the way from the hotel to the ground. He would use his watch to make the same movement over and over again, making me laugh. 'We'll win today,' he would say, again and again. 'We'll win today.' Whenever we passed the hospital, my line was, 'Yeah, Wiese, you've been here already, what with your kidney problems.' 'Yeah, super,' he'd reply. 'We'll win today, we'll win today.' It was on loop once a fortnight. 'We'll lose today,' came the prediction whenever I missed my cue. I had to apologise immediately and repeat my lines. Tensions ran high, especially before home games, during these short bus trips

– fifteen, twenty minutes through town, always down the same route. In moments like this, a degree of ease did us good. It was nice having Tim by my side, and I think he was thinking the same. We assured each other to a certain extent. Tim was one of the few teammates with whom I was really close. I could always count on his support and still keep in touch with him today. The same goes for Clemens Fritz. We shared a room for five years, which was more pleasant for me than it was for him. He complained about how I would fall asleep instantly, seconds after saying goodnight, the evening before games, 'like a pharaoh, arms crossed on his belly'.

It annoyed him that I always managed to drop off while he tossed and turned in his bed, not to mention my twitching leg making the duvet rustle. However, after night games, when the adrenaline took its time trickling out of my body, and I was immensely relieved to have left the game behind me and grateful that I wouldn't have to think about football for the next two or three days, I struggled to find peace of mind. Sometimes, my brain would only turn off at five in the morning, so training the next day was off the table. I upheld the friendship with Clemens, even after moving to London. To this day, we do business together running a property company. As a team, you're always trying to form a unit, a functioning structure, but after fifteen years in the game, you'll only take around three genuine friends on into the next stage of life. That's revealing about what football gives, or at least what it doesn't.

The first time I played for Werder was during a Champions League game against title holders Barcelona: Samuel Eto'o, Ronaldinho, Messi. It ended 1-1. Champions League matches were definitely a highlight, and each year we played at least one stunner. The other teams often underestimated us and didn't take us seriously. What a small place, they'd think after landing at a tiny airport and arriving at their hotel five minutes later. But then, the floodlights were turned on at the old Weserstadion, the one with the running track. Our incredible team spirit and the support of our fans, paired with absolute conviction and attacking football that captivated everybody, allowed us to overpower some very strong opponents. That season, our group consisted of Barcelona, Chelsea, and Levski Sofia. When Chelsea came to visit, under the lead of José Mourinho, they perished. I pushed past Didier Drogba and thumped a header home: 1-0 after a Frings corner, after which Drogba was substituted. For a centre-half, watching the opposing centre-forward leave the pitch is always a small victory. But my joy didn't last: Andriy Shevchenko came on for Drogba, followed by Arjen Robben half an hour before the end. I was knackered and couldn't really run anymore, but the crowd carried us to victory. At home, we were usually very good, especially in the Bundesliga. On good days, we played well enough to beat anyone. No one liked coming to Bremen, in part due to the Derby Star ball used during home games. There was something to that thing; it was a little heavier, a little firmer. It was easier to gauge where it might go, no swirling balls in sight.

During my time in Bremen, I was often visited by friends from back in Hannover and the Harz. They knew we were likely to win home games, which meant we could go out afterwards. In five years, they came to ten home games, and ten times we were able to properly celebrate and spend some quality time with each other. The public were understanding. It was a secret arrangement: as long as we were winning, we were allowed out. Often after our victories, people would bump into Werder players out on the town. It was inevitable due to the city's negligible size, but at the same time, it was part of its special charm. We went to the fair, the marksmen's festival, or a Bavarian beer tent, enjoying the atmosphere while being surrounded by the fans. There wasn't really a place for private celebrations. You were approachable, mixing with people and sharing the bar with supporters. *Modernes* opened its rooftop terrace at midnight, letting in the fresh air, and everyone – players and fans alike – sang the Werder anthem. I can't imagine something like that happening at many other Bundesliga clubs. Even acquaintances who had nothing to do with either the town or the club were always extraordinarily comfortable in this cosy environment.

Still, we knew to behave ourselves, because Thomas Schaaf had spies everywhere. He was on speaking terms with the owners of every bar and club, so we made sure to stay out of trouble. Trips to the cinema during the week were okay, as were parties on Saturdays a week before the next match. Getting hungover during the week or two days before a game definitely wasn't. There were players who frequented casinos a little too often and eventually got themselves barred after consultations with the club. One or two overdid it with the parties. But Schaaf never had to call the squad to order. I can't remember him ever punishing us collectively for going out. If we won, he tolerated it. I was very strict with myself, only going out after wins. I had no desire, nor any justification, to paint the town red after losing or drawing: I stayed home and didn't show my face anywhere.

Football is great fun and, at a certain level, comes with great financial security. You get to see the world and meet many exciting people. But at the same time, football is a profession, and just like in any other job, there are things that are less fun which can't be changed. Certain behaviours are simply taboo. There are stop signs; you can't take liberties. Which, at the end of the day, made it so much more pleasant to enjoy the fruits of your labour reasonably. Work hard, play hard, as they say. When you keep your nose to the grindstone, you've earned the right to put your best foot forward at the bar every now and then. A footballer's life is extremely strict, extremely intense, and demands a lot of discipline, but you do need your time off.

The first two years at Werder coincided with my relatively short time as a single man, and things did get steamy at times. Footballers were interesting to women, that wasn't a secret. It wasn't like a bunch of forty women came at you screaming, but Werder players attracted a lot of attention. I wasn't the type to have fifty one-night-stands, though, and there were no unhealthy rivalries or people competing with each other on the team, either. We just had fun together. That was our priority. It was never about who could drink more or who could get off with more women. Those weren't relevant considerations for us.

It's cool when people recognise you in the street, but you have to be able to cope with that kind of attention. Really, deep down, you and your teammates just want to be left in peace, away from prying eyes and, most importantly, away from judgement. *What is he drinking? How much is he drinking? Why is he drinking?* Bremen wasn't the worst when it came to this, because people kept their distance. I never had genuinely negative experiences there, never stayed home after a victory for fear of being monitored. After all, these boys nights out can get out of hand; anything can happen when blood alcohol levels rise too far, but I never found myself getting into fights or anything like that. This was mainly because the potential for conflict was low, as I only went out after good results and never encountered disappointed fans. I was never confronted with phrases like, 'What are you doing here? Shame on you, go home!' Some people are aggressive drunks, but rather than turning into a thug, I turn into a dancer. When you're tall, it can look unorthodox, but I really didn't care. One or two glasses of vodka ahoj, and I was in my very own world, blissfully unaware of the stares.

I was only ever late for an appointment once. We had won on Saturday, and I was due for a massage at ten o'clock the next morning. I had been drinking through the night and ended up oversleeping, something that had never happened to me before. A mate woke me with a phone call, and I rushed to the training ground. Holger Berger, our masseur, took one look at my face and understood at once. He kept it to himself, thank God. It was my only transgression at Werder. Apart from that, my dependability was rewarded with the job of DFB doping commissioner.

While most of the squad were checked in consultation with the club, the internationals had to be available for testing around the clock. NADA, the German anti-doping agency, required a daily record of their whereabouts. Players had to indicate their place and time of training and sleeping, whether they took the car to get to training, and so on. Back then, smartphones and apps weren't as common; everything was done via a website with personal logins. It was a very complex and serious matter. If the data wasn't entirely correct, NADA issued a warning. The worst-case scenario was a suspension over several years after three warnings. In order to facilitate this very elaborate process, I collected the relevant data every month with help of the massage staff and fed it into the system. I didn't take full responsibility, of course, but everyone was pleased that I was attending to the matter. Among the internationals, our programme was often identical, because the same procedures and appointments were scheduled for all of us, so the effort required was negligible. It was important to me that the task was performed accurately, which was why I did it myself.

I was a confidante, because I liked getting involved and taking care of things that might otherwise have been ignored or forgotten. As a result, I was admitted to the team committee quite quickly, without pushing the matter: it just happened. As an international, I was tested by examiners unannounced up to ten times a year, in addition to the spot checks. Occasionally, they even came to my house at five o'clock in the morning. While I didn't find this disruptive, it made it difficult to move about freely: spontaneous trips or holidays were forbidden. After retiring from international football, I no longer had to relay my whereabouts and was only required to give a random sample once a season. Compared to other elite sports, that is a relatively lax system, which occasionally leads the public to question, justifiably, whether it isn't prone to exploitation. The few positive cases I witnessed had at their centre banned substances contained in hair-restoring remedies and so, I think, were taken inadvertently rather than deliberately to improve performance. I might be too trusting, but in all the years in the Bundesliga, Champions League, the Premier League, and the big tournaments with the national team, I never had the feeling that someone on the other team was running suspicious lengths or unnaturally fast. On the contrary: long after someone was caught, I often wondered quietly how little difference it had actually made to their game. Neither fitness coaches nor doctors ever turned up with any funny potions or injections that would have stirred up doubt in my mind. The only thing I refused now and then were flu jabs during the season — I was afraid they would weaken my body too much — and the taking of creatine, a legal compound used to build up muscle. It worked very quickly to add two kilos of mass. In my mind there is no way that was healthy. Besides, there was a theory that creatine made your muscles more injury prone.

On some days, football plunged all of Bremen into a state of entirely legal intoxication. We descended upon opposing teams like a force of nature: I remember an 8-1 against Arminia Bielefeld, an amazing display on my twenty-fourth birthday. A year later, in September 2008 in Munich, we were 5-0 ahead, finishing 5-2. Tim Borowski, who was playing for Bayern at the time, scored both consolation goals. They went by like a dream, those years. At odds with his gruff exterior, Thomas Schaaf was a football romantic, a moustached high priest of attacking football. A 3-0 lead wasn't enough; he wanted goals, many, many goals. 'On and on and on' was his command. Werder's game relied heavily on the offensive: playing attractive attacking football was in Schaaf's DNA; he never strayed from the concept. As a defender, I sometimes thought there were quite a few opposition players running towards me, and that my team could have fallen back a bit more. Our diamond in midfield with only one defensive midfielder allowed the other team to outnumber us, especially towards the end of the game when players weren't working quite as hard. As a result, we conceded too many on one or two occasions, but the coach never minded. Schaaf preferred a 5-4 win to a 1-0 one, which was why the people of town were all the more proud of the team. Everyone knew the defence didn't have an easy life in that system, often left isolated and alone. We weren't made scapegoats; on the contrary, our work was held in high regard. Naldo and I were one of the best pairs in the league and we attracted a lot of praise.

As long as the results were just about okay, and we continued to qualify for European competitions, the press and public weren't critical. It was a golden age under Schaaf, beginning with a DFB-Pokal win in 1999 and culminating with the double in 2003/04. Schaaf and Klaus Allofs had built a genuinely top team with the ability to play some of the best football in the country. There was a feeling of deep satisfaction spreading through the city: *we're Werder Bremen, we're a family, we embody great football*. It was a unique combination, and which other German club could say that of themselves back then?

Towards the end of the 2006/07 season, I needed knee surgery. My joint had started to make a clicking sound for no reason. Click, click, click, I couldn't move my leg. They diagnosed a meniscal tear, and bam, I was back in the recovery system. Müller-Wohlfahrt referred me to Dr Boenisch in Augsburg, who removed the frayed piece of tissue. Then, six weeks of rehab in Donaustauf. I was back on my feet for the final two games of the season and the early summer internationals. Werder finished third, qualifying again for the Champions League ahead of Bayern, who, for the first time in two decades, didn't make the cut.

Schaaf's training camps on Norderney were legendary, or – rather – infamous. He had us working hard. Really, really hard. Beach runs at seven in the morning, followed by training at ten and then again in the afternoon. We were made to run back to the hotel, which meant a lot of pain for me: patella tendon, Achilles tendon, you name it; I managed to tweak them all. But that was his method. He wanted to show his squad what it meant to work hard in hostel-like accommodation without wifi, without a spa, without a sauna, without ice baths. The only pastime was dropping onto your bed at night. Every day was the same: get up at six thirty, mount your bike, and ride it to the beach. Schaaf's approach packed quite the punch. Fortunately, though, in my three years at Werder, I only had to endure it twice, because international duty meant longer summer holidays for me.

During the winter break, we generally went to Belek and once even to Dubai. Turkey in early January was always warmer than Bremen, but the weather was changeable. Some days, it would rain so hard that training had to be cancelled, which didn't upset anyone too much. The tournaments we played there were marred by the local referees who made some very strange decisions. But while some of the results were odd, they were only friendlies. Our evenings were spent almost exclusively inside the resort. Training was Schaaf's top priority; only once in a blue moon were we allowed to enjoy ourselves out on the town. We played a lot of poker in Belek, and a few young players thought they could keep up. That's another one of those phenomenons of professional football: as soon as there was some money on the table, they wanted to prove their courage, trying to make their mark as daredevils. It often ended rather badly for them.

During my second season, we had to win our final game against Bayer Leverkusen in order to qualify for the Champions League. Ten minutes before the end, Markus Rosenberg made it 1-0, dumping Leverkusen out of the European places. The BayArena descended into misery. After the final whistle, though, Carsten Ramelow, who was retiring after 333 Bundesliga games, stood in front of the remaining fans and was met with loud cheers and there were even a few tears. The result didn't matter any more. The scene was quite surreal, seeing as we were out of our minds on the other side of the pitch, celebrating Champions League qualification with our euphoric fans. They wouldn't let us leave for the dressing room, calling us back again and again. We didn't want it to stop, this joy of having accomplished something together: our supporters were full of energy, endlessly grateful for this amazing feeling, and a few feet along, a veteran was showered with sincere thanks for his life's work. Hold on to this moment, I told myself, don't forget this feeling. Life in football went by so fast that I knew I was going to have neither the time nor the mental capacity to reflect adequately on the beauty of such a moment.

After the 2008 Euros in Austria and Switzerland, I went on holiday for three weeks. During the warm-up on the first day back in training, I heard my knee again. *Click, click, click.* Again, no one had touched me. Again, I had damaged my left meniscus. It was frightening, because I realised my body hadn't been ready. I had played through an entire season followed by an international tournament, and now my body was on strike after three weeks off. The thought of pre-season preparation and a whole year ahead had put such a strain on my mind that my body reacted with a firm 'no'. It reclaimed the time it needed to recover properly from an exhausting year, literally bringing me to my knees. And so, back to the routine: an examination with Müller-Wohlfahrt, surgery with Boenisch in Augsburg, then rehab in Donaustauf. Apparently, an annual injury was part of my life now.

The best thing about time spent in rehab is meeting athletes from other sports, athletes who work eight times as hard as you for one percent of your wages. It was very interesting to talk to and exercise with people from beach volleyball, basketball, badminton, tennis, or athletics. I got to know many people very well, even though for a footballer, the environment wasn't the easiest in the beginning. Footballers had a reputation for arrogance with other athletes, who needed convincing in the beginning: you needed to show them that you were down to earth and able to carry a normal conversation. Not all of us were the same.

Until then, I had never had anything to do with women's handball, but that was about to change. Drastically. One of the players who was in rehab with me was incredibly good looking. She was athletic, self-confident — I fancied her at first sight. I had the feeling, though, that her first impression of me was far less spectacular, mainly because the pair of white compression stockings I was wearing didn't make me feel quite as sexy as usual. At least they were good for breaking the ice. Ulrike didn't know me, but she came up to me regardless, asking if I'd had surgery on both my knees. I was only wearing the other stocking as a precautionary measure.

I went straight to Klaus Eder to find out her age, to see if we might be compatible. Born in 1984, he said. Just like me. It was a green light. This could work, I thought. I was attracted to her: physically, of course, but more on a personal level. She was bold and didn't mince her words; the fact that I was a successful international footballer didn't phase her. Her self-confidence and athletic ambition impressed me immensely; she was smart, funny, a breath of fresh air. It was clear from day one that we were compatible.

Unfortunately, Ulrike didn't exactly have a high opinion of my job. 'I know footballers; they're arrogant,' she said. She played professional handball for HC Leipzig and had become acquainted with some lower-league players from Sachsen Leipzig and Lok Leipzig. They were brash boys, always aggressively on the pull, and not her cup of tea. I was desperate to convince her that this stereotype didn't apply to all footballers.

We ended up talking about the one thing we knew we had in common: injuries. She had suffered a cruciate rupture during the qualifying round for the Olympic Games in Beijing and had been sent to Donaustauf at the recommendation of Nadine Baum, HC Leipzig's physiotherapist. As a handball player, she didn't enjoy my advantage of having all therapists and individual treatments paid for. Where I was given four treatments a day, she was only entitled to one. For every week spent in rehab, she had to submit a separate medical report to her union and fight tooth and nail to have her costs paid.

She was almost back on her feet after a few months and she realised how much she was profiting from professional therapy. As a result, she wanted to stay a little longer — and to spend more time with me, I hope. In Germany, regardless of their type, professional athletes are only paid their full salary for the first six weeks of their injury. After that, the unions take over, but only in case of an accident, not for wear and tear, and only up to a maximum of €6,000 a month. It's a rule that still exists to this day. For Bundesliga players, that generally means heavy losses. There are private insurance companies, but their policies are extremely expensive. As a result, professionals are under major pressure to return after six weeks, or rather have their doctors certify them fit for work. But fit for what, exactly? Does it mean you're able to rejoin training or you're able to play a full game? And who ends up paying for your treatment, the club or your union? Perceptions differ, and there are many different regulations. In Germany, being injured as a professional footballer is a challenge: it can lose you a lot of money. Many aren't aware of this risk and, as a result, don't safeguard themselves properly. Fortunately, I was never out for more than six weeks in the Bundesliga. In England, by contrast, clubs pay out wages for a year and a half, which, especially for older or injury-prone players, makes a big difference. There, going into rehab isn't a problem at all, because you're able to bear all the costs yourself.

Ulrike's daring, foolhardy nature gripped me from the day we met. As a reasonably successful footballer, you're living in a bubble: everyone pats you on the back, everyone's pleased to see you. Ulrike, on the other hand, didn't look up to me. She was completely unimpressed and contradicted me a lot. That's someone at your eye level, I thought, you're on a level playing field with her. I wanted to know more, to be closer to her. After a few days in Donaustauf, we became companions in recovery; eating together, training together, supporting each other. Before we knew it, we were an actual couple. I wanted to ease into the relationship. As a footballer, you're somewhat relaxed in that respect: you flirt for a bit, then take it from there. But Ulrike wouldn't allow that. Eventually, she confronted me: 'What's the story here? Are you going to be a typical footballer about this? Enjoy yourselves for a bit while you're bored, then see me off? I don't think so. Tell me now: is this going somewhere?' I swallowed hard. 'Yeah, I can see it going somewhere,' I gulped.

At the end of her two-week stay, Ulrike's mobility was almost back completely. Her tear had healed, the muscles had regenerated, and she was back on the attack. On the last day, her parents picked her up. She introduced me, and her father took me aside. 'Do you even know what you're getting yourself into?' he asked. 'My daughter is petulant and moody. You live in Bremen, we live in Leipzig. How is this supposed to work?' I was perplexed; I hadn't been expecting an interview so soon.

After a few days together, Ulrike and I wanted to try a long-distance relationship. Sometimes, she came to Bremen; sometimes, I drove to Leipzig — three hours in the car each way. For a while, Hannover was our middle ground, an hour away from my place, two from hers. It was a tiring few months. She was a full-time professional, part of the national team, and was training to be a German and geography teacher. As a result, the weekends were off limits, so we generally met on Thursdays. But things couldn't continue this way. We decided to take the relationship to the next level and move in together — a step that might take others a little longer, but we thought it was time. Even her father couldn't dissuade me; I'm glad I didn't listen to him.

The solution to our situation was VfL Oldenburg. Back then, their women's handball team played in the first division, which was convenient: Ulrike signed with them in the summer in order to live with me in Bremen, and because she was still under contact in Leipzig, Oldenburg paid €18,000 in transfer fees. We moved into a flat in Bremen, and she regularly drove to Oldenburg for training and matches, less than an hour away. Ulrike earned €2,000 net a month, which was good money for women's handball at the time. In mid-2010, we decided to start a family. Our wish for a child was granted quickly and our first son, Paul, was born in Bremen in April 2011.

Because it's where I met Ulrike, 2008 rehab was the best ever. But at the same time, I was worried about the future of my career. Was it really normal to be so regularly sidelined? Was this an inevitable consequence of the grind of being a professional footballer? Did you practically have to sacrifice your body, was that the deal? I decided for myself to take the meniscal tear on the first day of training as a warning sign. I had put in more effort, extend my everyday life beyond post-match massages and regular treatment. Miro Klose advised me to consider insoles and recommended an orthopaedic centre.

'Have a look,' he said. 'They'll improve your running style. It'll make everything better.' You have to listen to those with experience who have your back, so I trusted Miro. They conducted a treadmill analysis, and a slow-motion replay showed my pelvis collapsing with every step, forcing my back to compensate. It wasn't noticeable in real time. 'You definitely need insoles,' said Jens Asendorf, head of the department. 'And we'll have a personal trainer build up your muscles, because you need better protection. Unfortunately, football is a running sport, and moving your long limbs this much is going to do long-term damage.'

It made sense and I was hooked. The centre referred me to Jacek and Tomek, fitness coaches whose studios were close to the Weserstadion. They were Polish and hard as nails. Following the cool down session we had at the club the day after each home game I would pay Jacek and Tomek a visit, so usually once a week, sometimes twice. Strictly speaking, you were supposed to lessen the burden on game day. That time was meant for recovery, but I ramped up my body: ninety minutes of stabilisation exercises, using only my own body weight. Mark Verstegen and his team of experts, introduced to the national team by Jürgen Klinsmann, did similar things, but they were considerably more complicated, with rubber straps, sledges, and so on. In Bremen, while very basic, the exercises for gut, back, legs, and bottom were exhausting. I lay on the floor, moving my leg up and down forty times, followed by the same in a new position until I cramped. Forty times up and down with my gut, forty times up and down with my hips. Forty seconds of stretching, forty seconds of holding the position. It was hardcore, almost like a military drill.

In the beginning, I was sure I wasn't going to make it, but I hadn't reckoned with my coaches. They motivated me immensely: one was next to me, accompanying me through each exercise with encouragement, the other gave me a bollocking whenever I got in the wrong position or tried to give up. After a while, I began to notice the benefits. Standing on balance boards to train the small muscles in my knee, for example, I could feel an increase in stability. Finally, they made me do active stretching exercises, extending my thigh muscles as far as they would go. I returned from showering fully charged: knackered, of course, but with the feeling of improvement. I managed to recover more quickly after games, too, which was a completely new experience for me. Ever since my ankle surgery following the 2006 World Cup, I had never been completely free from pain; the area had always been tender. The orthopaedist softened my boots at the heel to ease the pressure on my Achilles tendon. At last, I could run pain free. We also continued regular treadmill analysis to check the effect of both the training and the insoles. It was plain to see that my running style had changed for the better and that my hips had become more stable, meaning my back and legs no longer had to compensate as much. My legs were running straighter and with more balance, which increased my ability to cushion the strains of the game. On the whole, I felt much less exhausted between matches. I challenged my body and invested time and money: ten sessions a month cost €3,000 — a reasonable amount for a professional, considering the positive effect. To me, it was definitely worth the money. They say your body is an asset, but how much do you really work towards that? How much thought do you put into that at the beginning of your career? I had no idea how great a difference such a small amount of extra effort could make.

My closest friends on the team, whom I told about the session in confidence, were stunned: 'Three thousand euros a month? Far too much money. And anyway, there's a gym at the club!' But Werder, with only two coaches, couldn't have offered me this kind of individual, intense training. I needed that impulse from outside, though, and so I kept going until my farewell in the summer of 2011.

The process didn't protect me completely from injury. In 2009, after a foul by Ivica Olić during a match against Hamburg, the ligaments in my ankle tore yet again, but rather than a reaction to chronic overload or incorrect positioning, it was an accidental impact injury. Werder knew nothing of my secret special training. There are various theories on the best methods of inter-game regeneration, and the club did want the players to do a thing on the day after a match: cool down, massage, then home. Some did a little weight training. Werder only got wind of my programme towards the end, after three years, and ultimately didn't approve. But it was too late: with its short distances between my flat, the stadium, the training ground, and the fitness studio, Bremen offered perfect conditions for me to work harder than ever on my physical foundations.

2008/09 was defined by our northern rivalry with Hamburg. We played them four times in three mad weeks: once in the league, twice in the UEFA Cup semi-finals, and once in the semi-finals of the DFB-Pokal. We came away successful every time; I scored from close range during the cup game at the Volksparkstadion. It was during the second leg of the UEFA Cup semi-final that I twisted my ankle in that duel with Olić, who stepped on my leg afterwards and caught me at such an unfortunate angle that all lateral ligaments snapped. I was sidelined for both finals. We lost to Shakhtar Donetsk but won the German Cup: 1-0 against Leverkusen, my first trophy. The joy in Bremen was overwhelming; never before had I seen a town rejoice like that. The route from the airport to the town hall balcony was lined with what felt like a hundred thousand people. I couldn't believe how many of them had come out, or how happy and grateful they were.

You have to appreciate the fact that you can grant others such joyous moments with minimum effort. Every season, you have to be mindful of the hamster wheel: you're focused so intensely on the next game that you risk neglecting important factors. Football is Germany's most popular sport. Almost everyone has some sort of interest in it, which is why there's so much money in the game. It's why players, coaches, officials, and agents have such high salaries. We're not just paid to play, but to bring joy to the people. Meeting children, recording video messages, and simply being there to sign autographs even during training surrounded by thousands of fans — that's our job. A photo, an autograph, maybe a kind word, it really doesn't take much to make kids happy. As happy, in fact, as I was when Ingo Anderbrügge gave me five seconds of his time.

If the children are happy, so are the parents. Whenever I had the feeling during my career that I wanted to be left alone, I got my act together and remembered how my life and my job involve the obligation to thank people adequately for their support and affection. My parents' words rang in my ears again and again. 'Be glad. Just be glad you're in this position.' Right at the beginning of my professional career, they had insisted I handle all mailed autograph requests myself. I didn't always feel like it and, occasionally, I just didn't have the time. I would catch myself procrastinating and leaving some letters lying around for a bit longer. I wanted peace and quiet, but it never took long for my guilty conscience to get the better of me. You can't run from doing the right thing. Most fans wanted autograph cards, but many also sent Panini stickers, Topps Match Attax trading cards, photographs, or shirts, anything that could be signed. I never received any underwear from female admirers, but fans from China and Japan liked to send me hand-drawn pictures. There were many requests for charity events: signed shirts were auctioned off, because even a few hundred euros can sometimes go a long way. That was also one of the reasons why I started my own foundation in 2006. I had realised how easy it was to raise money for a good cause, and I had the means to do it. A driver always dropped me off at training, I was wearing good workout clothes and a selection of boots: there are many who aren't as lucky, but I wasn't aware of that back then. Today, I'm delighted that we can make a big difference on a small scale. I believe we're duty-bound to make this nowhere-near-perfect world a slightly better place.

After the Olić-induced ligament tear, usual protocol followed: Müller-Wohlfahrt, surgery, Donaustauf. I was surrounded by my usual circle of doctors, physios, and coaches, and felt well looked after. The injury had happened towards the end of 2009/10, so I was back on my feet in time for the new season. Winning the German Cup meant we had qualified for the UEFA Cup, but in the league we had only finished tenth. A small downwards trend was looming. Werder, who over the years had managed to replace departing stars with great cunning in the market, were out of luck. In addition, the money available for transfers and salaries had to be adjusted downwards: the twenty million euros that were missing due to our failure to qualify for the Champions League left a big hole in the budget. The result was an unavoidable loss of quality. Big stars were now sold even more quickly without being properly replaced. It was a vicious circle: no Champions League participation meant no money to assemble a team fit for the Champions League. 2009/10 was the last time we managed to defy this creeping process: with a huge effort, we managed to finish third and scrape into the tournament. But it was clear that the high turnover of players combined with the increasingly narrow financial parameters would inhibit the team's performance level. It was inevitable.

After the 2010 World Cup in South Africa, Mesut Özil was the next top player to leave the club. I indicated to Klaus Allofs that I, too, was considering saying my farewells. Arsenal had signalled their interest, and I was very tempted. The Gunners had been on my mind since the days of Aunt Ute in Plymouth, and now, for the first time, the Premier League was in reach. *You could make it this year*, I thought. I had already pushed myself far, had already achieved more than I thought my skills would allow, so I wanted to grasp that opportunity. I wanted international experience, without knowing what that meant or what it entailed: I was desperate to give it a go. England was my aim. But that summer, Klaus Allofs didn't want to lose two key players.

'There's no way we're letting you go,' he declared. 'You've got another two years on your contract.' I accepted his decision, and we played a terrible season. Chucked out of the Champions League in the first round, we didn't even manage to finish third in a group with Inter, Tottenham, and FC Twente. Things were even worse in the league. We lost game after game, 4-0 at Schalke, 6-0 at Stuttgart. At home, with the ground being converted, we'd lost the old atmosphere and were no longer feared by other teams. At Christmas, we were only four points from the relegation places and finally had to acknowledge that we were, in fact, fighting to stay up. I was familiar with the situation from my time at Hannover, but in Bremen we were completely unprepared. In the beginning, the goal had been to play at Champions League level again. Now, after a few months, the aim was to avoid games against Rot-Weiß Oberhausen or Erzgebirge Aue the next year. As a team who were used to winning most of their games, we struggled to cope with the constant setbacks. The boss was discontented, the players were discontent, and the fans didn't understand what on earth was going on. What had happened to their beloved club? The usual strategies no longer worked, but we didn't know why. We couldn't find our way out of this downward spiral and felt, if you'll pardon the expression, like shit. We were failing both our club and our town. Over the course of this fiasco, emotions ran high; everyone was on edge.

Marko Arnautović vented his spleen in front of live cameras. 'What a dump,' he spat during training one day, when the whole team had been ordered back to the dressing room for a meeting. His skills were outstanding, but his eccentric manner made it difficult for him to integrate. People were as much puzzled by the white wall he had built around his house as they were by his decision to stitch 'Champions League winner 2010' onto his boots despite not having played a single Champions League minute for Inter the year before. In the dressing room, he went by 'Astro', a nickname born from his tendency to be miles away. For the most part, Astro was all right if maybe a little immature, and our plight was certainly not all his fault. Attempts to back difficult characters who had failed elsewhere was part of the trade at Bremen. Many of these complex personalities fulfilled their full potential in this quiet, considerate environment: Ailton, for instance, could only function at Werder. But during the fight against relegation, these individuals found their eccentricities weren't forgiven as readily. If you remove yourself from the collective by choice, you'll be the first to stand in the rain without an umbrella.

There were a few crisis meetings, in which Thomas Schaaf demanded each player express their own views on the situation. Twenty-five different ideas and explanations. He and Allofs listened to them all impassively, then said, 'They're great, these stories of yours. But everyone's tale is about someone else. Not one of you has said a word about how *you* might improve the situation. Not one of you has taken time to himself and said, "This is where I messed up!" If you're going to keep putting the blame on others rather than giving your own performances some thought, we might as well forget about the whole thing!'

Schaaf's speech made us realise how much footballers struggle with criticism. It was always someone else's fault. We had to change the way we thought about things. Schaaf also scheduled extensive post-match debriefings. We watched entire recordings, sometimes even twice in a row. He would pause, wind back and forwards, and explain our mistakes as long as it took for everyone to understand them. And then *again*, just in case. He was rigorous; sometimes, we would sit together for three hours.

Schaaf wanted *everyone* to understand what he was asking of them, and, unfortunately, that took time. While I personally thought of it more as a help than an imposition, it was also a type of punishment. Some players had left school fifteen years ago, so they weren't used to sitting in a chair for two hours listening to a lecture. It annoyed them: engaging with their job for three hours every day was already too much to ask. But Schaaf knew exactly what he was doing. This form of, let's call it constructive toughness, was what we needed. Every manager has their own methods and, sometimes, punishment is necessary to effect real change. Footballers like to brush off negative things and often take the path of least resistance, but Schaaf showed us in no uncertain terms that this approach had consequences.

Those never-ending reviews made you scrutinise your own

performance more intensely and stop the practice of blaming defeats on weak excuses. The ability to take criticism is a major talking point in football. No one wants to be exposed in front of their peers; in this respect, professional players are no different to kids at school. You feel naked, unprotected. You fear for your reputation and your position in the pack. Criticism hurts, much more so than a kick to the shin, but the trick is understanding that while things are meant personally, they're not malicious. It's when the manager stops talking to you or even about you that you know you're in danger, because even if harsh words are used, the very fact they are criticising you is a sign they're still counting on you and are trying to help. Of all my time in Bremen, the 2010/11 season was both the most unpleasant and the most educational.

You couldn't have fitted a sheet of paper between the squad and the fans. That season, though, the crowd's love turned to disappointment: they couldn't understand why their team was at the wrong end of the table. Many thought it was due to a lack of effort, because there was definitely enough skill. Others suspected the wealthy footballers didn't care about the supporters' sorrows. You had to put up with people asking critical questions in the street or at the training ground. A lot was being linked specifically to the defence, to me — which, after years of success, was a major adjustment. But there wasn't only negative feedback, not by a long shot. Fans also spared some encouraging words: 'Don't give up, it'll be fine.' A number of autograph hunters stuck by us, keeping faith regardless of results. I had various encounters that all furthered me in their own way. In London, I missed this kind of contact and communication with the fans: as a player, you were completely isolated there.

In those dark Bremen days, the way we liaised with the members of the press changed, too. The straightforward accessibility that distinguished a professional's life became slightly unpleasant: virtually every day, the training ground car park turned into a mixed zone, with reporters crowding in and asking for comments on the current negative mood. They knew to intercept you between pitch and dressing room, too. You were effectively surrounded, it was open season — which is fine when you're winning game after game. After defeats, though, things look very different. You're walking around in a terrible mood, getting on your own nerves, and are still supposed to be telling the press something reasonably intelligent. 'Sorry, not today,' sometimes resulted in journalists snarking at you, which was fine: at the end of the day, the situation was hard on them, too. Most of them were Werder fans themselves and suffered like we did under the collapse. We had to worry almost until the end but managed to stay up after 2-0 win at home against Borussia Dortmund. Under Jürgen Klopp, they had won the league a week before, and some clearly had been enjoying themselves in the days after. They could barely complete a pass between them and we won the game easily, putting an end to this awful season.

That summer, I was made captain. Without continental football, though, the club still needed to earn money from transfers, so the idea of a transfer wasn't off the table. Klaus Allofs made it clear that he would agree to a sale for ten million euros. I took him by his word: in Bremen, an oral agreement was enough and there was no need to have it in writing. Roman was in contact with the Gunners, but a concrete offer from London was a long time coming, and so the 2011/12 season began. We were doing well: 2-0 against Kaiserslautern, 5-3 against Freiburg, 2-1 against Hoffenheim. Three wins in four games, one defeat (1-0 to Leverkusen), and third in the table, level on points with leaders Bayern. I braced myself for the fact that nothing would happen with regards to Arsenal, but then something did.

At Old Trafford, Manchester United beat Arsenal 8-2. A humiliation, to which the Arsenal fans reacted by rebelling against Arsène Wenger's cautious transfer policy. It was Sunday, 28 August 2011, and on that very night, my agent called to tell me Arsenal wanted to sign me after all. I went to see Klaus Allofs in his office to confirm that he would stand by our agreement. My dream of England, of Arsenal, was seemingly coming true three days before transfer deadline day, but at the same time, this unexpected turn was cause for reflection: I had only just been given the captain's armband, I'd only had it for four games. I struggled to say goodbye so suddenly and found it difficult leaving the club, the city, and my many trusted companions. It was a big step. On the other hand, following the successful start to the season, I no longer feared everything going south without me. With Clemens Fritz, my successor, the team would be in good hands. 'Clemens, you'll have to pick up the baton now,' I said. After five years of sharing a room, we had become very close friends.

Unfortunately, the era of the Bremen block on the national team had come to an end. Clemens, Torsten Frings, Tim Borowski, and Tim Wiese were no longer being considered by

Jogi Löw, Miro Klose had already signed with Bayern in 2007, and Mesut Özil was playing with Madrid. We had made the trips to international games together, always with the feeling of collective strength and pride in our club and its ability to keep pace with the big guns. It had been an extraordinary story.

The Bremen block on the national team was replaced primarily by Dortmund players, who became the counterpart to Bayern there. As of 2019 Werder don't have a current German international, and almost every year, the club is stuck in mid-table, sometimes even fighting to stay up. Thomas Schaaf and Klaus Allofs are long gone; they couldn't compensate for the continual departures and had no means of strengthening the squad adequately without extra income from international competitions. All that is left from the big moments are pleasant memories. Of course, a relegation battle does unite a team and, if the disaster is avoided, triggers feelings of tremendous happiness. But there was also the fact that for so long, Werder had stood for success and were now fighting for survival. It was sad to see how, in the space of just ten years, things had changed completely. Time and again, I am amazed by the pace at which football moves. It is my ardent wish that the good times return to the Weserstadion.

3

PREMIER LEAGUE

I WAS IN MY ROOM AT THE DÜSSELDORF HYATT
Regency, the national team hotel, when Arsène Wenger called.
He spoke to me in German, which impressed me straight away.
The line was crackling, but it had nothing to do with the connection: being contacted by such a distinguished manager was exciting. Wenger explained how he needed a player who would take
responsibility on the pitch, contribute his qualities, and identify
with the club. The only English word used in the conversation
was 'leadership'. I could imagine what he meant by that; his ideas
were very precise. 'Alright,' was all I needed to say in return.

Wenger could just as well have been reading me the menu at his favourite Alsatian restaurant, and it wouldn't have made a difference to me. I wanted to play for him, and his phone call only encouraged me. The transfer window was only open for another day, though, so we had to act fast. My situation was on a knife edge, so I asked Jogi Löw to allow me to fly to London for a few hours in order to do my medical, stressing how much I wanted this move.

It was a surreal episode, because I had no longer been expecting to be given this chance, and I was all the more determined to take it. Löw was very helpful, as were all of the DFB staff. He endorsed the transfer explicitly, telling me the move abroad would do me good. A driver picked me up from Heathrow airport and stopped the car at a typically English, suburban terraced house. I wondered if he had made a mistake. In Germany, you're given your pre-signing examination at large, modern hospitals. In contrast, the London clinic was tiny, a dollhouse with tight, winding rooms and not exactly state-of-the-art machinery. I spent five hours in the MRI scanner, lots of time to reflect, worry, and pray. *Please let everything be okay. I hope I get through; they'll have to wave me through. I hope my body — my capital — is good enough for them to really want me.* Afterwards, I was taken to the training ground, where Arsenal's physio wanted to take a look at my joints. I didn't see Arsène Wenger. Manuel Almunia and Sébastien Squillaci were sitting in the dressing room, but the rest of the squad wasn't there, they were away with their national teams.

Back in Düsseldorf, there was good news: I had passed. The contract was faxed to the provisional office the DFB had set up at the Hyatt. I signed it and sent it back. A year later and I could have gone on a free transfer, which most probably would have meant more money for me and Roman Pletz, but I didn't want to push my luck. It might have been done in passing, but the transfer was finally complete. After two international fixtures (6-2 against Austria, 2-2 in Poland), I returned to Bremen to pack my things. A few fans and journalists bade me farewell at the training ground. Given how I felt about the club, the city and the people after five years, the quick goodbye felt too hurried. Unfortunately, that isn't unusual in football: often, there's no time for the essentials.

I felt slightly uneasy before my first day, seeing as Arsenal had lost 8-2 to Manchester before the break. I was convinced there was trouble at the club. If Werder had suffered such a defeat against a league rival, there would been all kinds of fuss for the entire next week, with journalists and furious fans waiting at the training ground, readying themselves for crisis. I had just arrived at a new club, was I about to be subjected to that kind of stress immediately? It was my first thought, and it worried me. Had it not been for this spectacular defeat, Wenger might not have signed me at all, I thought, and that was disconcerting. Some English newspapers had labelled me a panic buy, which was why I braced myself for a difficult week under massive pressure.

It would be a matter of life and death from day one, so at first training, I wanted to prove my mentality, presence, and attitude. But in the end, things turned out different entirely. On that Thursday, many players hadn't yet returned from their travels with their national teams. Two days before the next match at home against Swansea, recovery was the only thing scheduled. We ran a few laps, did a few passing exercises, then went straight back to the dressing room. I was baffled. Over time, though, I learned that in England training is given less emphasis. Prior to Champions League games, we took a few steps around the hotel at best; there was no real session or even a warm-up. It took some getting used to, but I found it helpful: recovery just did more for me. Other than that, the procedures were similar to those in Germany, apart from the fact that tea, toast, and porridge were considered afternoon snacks.

Contrary to my expectation, an extensive review of *that* Manchester game didn't happen. Instead, the focus was entirely on the upcoming match. There was no feeling of tension, let alone crisis. Any negativity was blocked out — literally — due to the fact that London Colney – Arsenal's training ground – didn't admit fans or members of the press. For me, that was another big change. At Werder, when you arrived for training the day after a poor match, there would be five camera crews waiting. it immediately put you in a bad mood. *Great, now they're coming out of the woodwork.* When we were winning, there was no one waiting. But you couldn't just ignore them when they were there. A refusal to communicate would have been interpreted as a sign of weakness or moral cowardice: 'The team won't face up? The captain won't talk? Well, seems like none of them know what to do!'

English football culture is different in this regard. We were supposed to play, not talk. Apart from the manager, no one in the club commented on the situation. The team worked calmly as if nothing had happened. I wasn't introduced to the press either, which was fine by me. I wouldn't have made it far with my schoolboy English anyway. This way, I was able to take small steps, almost incognito. I didn't tell the story about Aunt Ute and the Arsenal shirt until later, when I was able to express myself more eloquently. Having an interpreter accompany me to interviews was out of the question. I had never been the type to do well with languages at school, but from day one, I was determined to communicate with both club and media in English only. I was going to make mistakes, of course, but I didn't care. It was the only way I could improve, the only way for people to see that I wasn't just passing through but was taking this seriously and was committed to my new life. That was one of the reasons, I think, why people were very open-minded towards me from the beginning. German efficiency was one of the phrases I encountered a lot. It clearly had positive connotations: Jens Lehmann had played for Arsenal for a long time and, to my benefit, left a good impression.

The general appreciation for our country was higher than I thought. English people associate us with competence; when they think of Germany, they think of cars, kitchens, and infrastructure. In their minds, I was the Volkswagen of centre-halves – solid and reliable, more substance than style. I worked constantly, quietly, and diligently, without airs and graces: I lived up to the cliché. Not only do you feel more German when you're abroad, you're also automatically made your country's ambassador, whether you like it or not. I was used to this representative role a little from my time with the national team, but it felt slightly more pronounced in England. The past, i.e. the First and Second World War, are very present in the public consciousness. Many jokes are made about the subject, but that only shows how seriously people still take it. It's something I learned over time: the British always approach the really important things with humour. A city like London will open your eyes to completely new perspectives. You meet new people, are confronted with new situations. London is a melting pot with amazing diversity. Our neighbours back then were Jewish. One day, they invited Ulrike and I for Shabbat. Blessings were recited before dinner, while my wife and I stood there looking at each other, unsure how to behave. The burden of history weighed on us. The family's grandparents had fled to England from Germany, but out of anger and grief over losing their home, they had never spoken another word of German. While they were recounting their history, our neighbours were perfectly normal and incredibly gracious. 'What happened is not your fault,' they said. It was moving; I was again made aware of how important it is to deal responsibly with the past.

Initially, being isolated from the outside world at London Colney was very pleasant. Super professional. You're able to focus on the essentials without having to worry about what car to drive, what clothes to wear, and how your decisions might be interpreted. *Might someone turn it into a story if I smile on the way to training even though we've lost a game?* In England, none of that mattered, because you're out of reach. There are no distractions whatsoever. In Germany, things are moving in a similar direction. More and more managers have their teams train, at least in part, behind closed doors. It stops upcoming opponents from gaining any insight into tactics and prevents unnecessary unrest. Nowadays, every little disagreement gets photographed and puffed up, even if it's cleared up within seconds. It costs both the club and manager a lot of energy that could be put to more sensible use. Security concerns also play an increasingly important role; unfortunately, there is a lot going on in this mad world. The 1972 Munich Olympics, the 2015 attacks in Paris, or the bombing of Borussia Dortmund's team bus: top athletes are often targeted, and training behind closed doors reduces potential risks, which is why, in England, the practice won't change. 'We have to be shielded, otherwise something could happen,' has become an ingrained mindset, and sadly, it has become worse over the years. More security staff are hired, and greater priority is given to personal protection. After our FA Cup win in May 2017, Arsenal cancelled the traditional open-top bus parade due to safety reasons. Two days before, a terrorist had blown himself up during an Ariana Grande concert in Manchester, killing 23 people, including many children.

But that kind of isolation has disadvantages too. There's a major difference between the sessions at a spa-like training ground and a game in front of a crowd of thousands, and for some youth players, it can be too much. In England, there is virtually no interaction with fans. If someone doesn't have the money for a ticket, they'll never get to see their team in person, which leads to players virtually being mobbed on the way out of the underground Emirates car park or the Colney gates. Every now and then, an autograph hunter will jump in front of your car. There is no normal interaction between players and people in the streets, which means you're hardly ever confronted with different perspectives, you never get to witness first-hand how much the club means to people, and only rarely do you have to speak to journalists. Without realising it, you suddenly only have dealings with people within the club. But it's important to face uncomfortable questions once in a while, too: in my opinion, players tend to give too little rather than too much to their profession. In the long run, preventing the public from gaining any kind of normal access to them doesn't do players any favours. Rather, it creates a vacuum for them to float around in. Living such a cloistered life isn't good for someone's development.

In Bremen, I enjoyed receiving direct feedback about the last game and how I played, be it from adults or children. It showed me how people saw me. I would find myself in situations where I said yes to many things and took pictures willingly, but sometimes, I refused. You were given the opportunity to express yourself, to tell people clearly what you wanted. In some cases, people would come up to me, shouting things like, 'Picture!' or 'Autograph!' In return, I would ask, 'Do you know how to construct a sentence?' or sometimes, 'Is that a question? Was that a request?' In England, a dialogue like this couldn't happen; clubs tend to show explicit disapproval. German clubs like Bremen, on the other hand, argue that access is part of their identity. 'We want people to buy the shirt from the fan shop and come to the training ground to get an autograph. That's who we are, that's our brand. That's Werder Bremen: we're open and informal. We don't hide.'

There is no such tradition of access and accountability in England, because clubs here aren't owned and controlled by their members. They're companies. Maybe they don't consider daily contact with supporters to be imperative, because tickets and broadcasting rights bring in enough money anyway.

In the days after the 8-2 defeat in Manchester, however, the ability to block out the outside world was an advantage to the team. Based on the relaxed atmosphere alone, no one would have thought that we had just suffered one of the most embarrassing defeats in the club's history, nor considered that our fans might burn down the stadium if we lost to newly-promoted Swansea City on Saturday. The English approach when it comes to access to training grounds differs so dramatically from what I experienced in Germany, that I can't really draw a comparison – I can't really say which was better or worse. Sometimes in London, I wished things were more like in Bremen, and sometimes in Bremen, I wished they were more like in London.

In 2011, there were no other Germans at Arsenal, nor any German speakers — apart from Wenger. Because he demanded I give instructions to my teammates, I had to learn the English technical vocabulary as fast as I could: left shoulder, right shoulder, man-on, etc. I wanted to integrate on a verbal level as quickly as possible. Every manager has his own sound, his own way of addressing a team. Wenger was very calm and factual; only very rarely would he raise his voice. Occasionally, he would tell us to smother opposition players 'like an anaconda', or chase the ball 'like a pack of wolves'. Lukas Podolski's response in the dressing room to the latter was a loud howl, which earned him an approving laugh from Wenger. For the most part, though, his phrases were much less flowery; big motivational speeches weren't in his nature. In the beginning, I used to translate every one of his sentences in my mind. I had to work out what exactly he meant and how I was to implement it. The video analysts showed us Swansea's strengths and weaknesses, but the emphasis of the theoretical preparation was very much on our own game. With the aid of clippings from the United match, it was made clear to us where we needed to improve and what we needed to do differently. Wenger's message was that we, with our way of playing football — fast, effective in combinations, variable in the attack — were absolutely superior to the other team. It was his fundamental conviction, from which everything else was derived. 'I trust you,' he said, again and again. 'I demand you give your all, but how exactly you realise things is up to you. I'm granting you many freedoms.'

Before the match, we went over set-pieces to see how we might organise ourselves, and I agreed the details with captain Robin van Persie. In the dressing room, we more than lived up to the German-Dutch football rivalry. Jokingly, he would call me 'bratwurst', one of the few German words he knew. In return, I referred to him as 'tulpe', German for tulip. These little verbal battles were funny and made the settling-in period go by swiftly; the transition was quick. Wenger, who had been at the helm since 1996 and had given the club a global identity with his visionary short passing, had nixed one of his fundamental principles for me. 'I will never sign a player who is taller than me,' the 6ft 2in Frenchman had promised a few years earlier.

Before my arrival, he didn't know me in person but still trusted me instantly as a German national player with a certain reputation for a clean, focused game. I didn't get the sense that he had any doubts or that he felt as if I had to prove myself. There are managers who do employ those psychological games, but Wenger isn't one of them. *I'm banking on you*, was the feeling I got from him. *You're doing your thing; you're helping the squad the way you are. Come what may, you'll cope with it. You'll learn a lot here.* In an interview with a French football magazine, he described his role as a facilitator. Wenger doesn't want to drill players and order them about, but rather make it possible for them to fulfil their potential. Instead of pushing them in a certain direction on their journey, he supports them down their own path. Thomas Schaaf later told me that he had talked to Wenger about me. I think it was a predominantly positive conversation. 'I portrayed you the way you are,' Schaaf said. Most likely, Wenger had formed his own opinion about me as a result, but I now had to live up to that image in my daily work.

On the day of the Swansea game, the atmosphere in the dressing room was relaxed and positive, with loud music coming from the speakers. The crowd, too, seemed to have forgotten their anger over the Old Trafford disgrace and were in good spirits. I was introduced to the concept of successful clearances being celebrated and tough tackles being met with applause. The appreciation for a won ball is more pronounced in England than it is in Germany; the cheering makes it sound as if a goal has been scored. Fans appreciate it if a player does the team's dirty work, preferably by thundering into tackles and taking man and ball. It wasn't really my style, but the crowd's encouragement supported me more than they knew.

Speaking up in front of my colleagues in my very first match was difficult for me. I didn't want to be the town crier but instead wanted to gain confidence in my own game through good, simple actions, then pass on that confidence. On the pitch, you don't make yourself heard with words: you need to deliver the goods first, or what you say counts for nothing. Play simple, win your tackles, draw out your opponent. That's what I had been trained to do and that had always been the core of my game. At Arsenal, I couldn't suddenly start spraying around fifty-yard passes. I preferred being effective. Time and again, you have to remember your strengths and weaknesses and play the way you know best, especially during your debut. The first impression is crucial. I wanted to prove to my teammates, the manager, and the crowd that Arsenal had signed a good player and not, to put it in the words of Robin van Persie, a bratwurst. Due to my height, there had been concerns before my arrival that I would be too slow for the team's back four, which pushed high up the field. Some fans had probably been wishing for another Tony Adams, a hard-as-nails fighter. My name likely meant little to them. Robbie Savage wasn't exactly thrilled, either. 'I don't rate Mertesacker at all,' he told BBC Radio 5 Live. 'He wasn't convincing at Real Madrid.' Savage had confused me with Christoph Metzelder.

My objective was to play in a way that instantly showed both teammates and fans my determination: I had come to London to advance the club, and I meant business. It worked out well to an extent; apart from a small mistake, I played a solid game.

Our overall performance wasn't very good, but we still won 1-0. Swansea 'keeper Michel Vorm's punt hit the back of Àngel Rangel's legs, and Andrey Arshavin just needed to slide to the ball into the empty goal. The important thing was that we had won and that had done so without conceding. After the United disaster and my own short pre-season, this was a good way for me to start the season with the Gunners.

Together with our son Paul, who was only a few months old, Ulrike was still living in Germany during those first days. Courtesy of the club, I was staying at The Grove in Hertfordshire just outside the city, the same hotel used by the England team before they played games at Wembley. Mikel Arteta lodged there too, which was why in the beginning, we used to drive to training together. He had come from Everton and was familiar with driving on the left-hand side of the road, so he played instructor for a while. Out of habit, some foreign players drive around town in their cars from the continent for years, meaning they find themselves on the wrong side at railway crossings and in multi-story car parks and so always need a passenger to press the button. I wanted to get myself a right-hand drive immediately, because I wasn't going to do things by halves. Taking the same route over and over again meant I got to grips with the system within a week, but even today, I don't enjoy unfamiliar roads. Steering is so very different: you take short turns to the left and long ones to the right, and against traffic. Everything is upside down. To top it off, Greater London isn't so much a city as it is a cluster of hundreds of villages with short, winding roads that were already too tight for stagecoaches two hundred years ago.

The Swansea match was followed by a Champions League trip to Dortmund. After dinner the night before the game, there suddenly came the cry of 'All the newbies have to sing!' I was prepared, I knew it was coming. I didn't want to humiliate myself by butchering the national anthem the way some players do; that wasn't the first impression I was going for. Even less significant moments like this are an opportunity to demonstrate the kind of person you are: it all comes down to the attitude you exhibit and whether you're able to carry your audience. I considered for a moment. What was a huge hit in Germany that contained some English words, something universally usable? In the end, I chose DJ Ötzi's 'Hey Baby'. I figured if I sang one or two verses and then dipped into the chorus, they should all be able to follow. Armed with a roll to use as a microphone, I climbed onto a chair. 'When I saw you walking down the street... She's so pretty, she's so fine, I wanna make her mine, oh mine...'

Before I knew it, everyone had joined in loudly. We had such fun; it went brilliantly. To this day, people say my performance belongs into Arsenal's all-time top three, and every summer until his departure in 2017, Kieran Gibbs told me how it had stuck in his memory. Arteta was good that night, too: he did the Macarena, causing Wenger and his coaching staff to roll around laughing. In my experience, the new generation, the ones that usually know how to be creative with music and smartphones, tend to struggle with recitals. Many of them don't quite manage to come out of their shells. The eternal number one of Arsenal's Got Talent, though, is Petr Čech. The Czech goalkeeper joined the club in 2015 and introduced himself with a freestyle rap. None of us had ever seen anything like it. He went from one table to the next, coming up with a verse for everyone. 'Mesut Özil and Per Mertesacker, you won the World Cup, and everyone thinks you're motherfuckers.' He proceeded to the staff table. 'Right here at the top, now I need to be careful, so I better stop.' We were stunned. It was brilliant. Čech had given the performance during a trip to China and repeated it in the Far East in 2017. He wanted to inspire the young players, show them what it meant to be creative and how to earn respect off the pitch. A move like that scored points with the rest of the team; it's not forgotten in a hurry. As a result, the quality of subsequent displays genuinely improved.

I wondered why I didn't have to attend the pre-game press conference ahead of the Dortmund game. Whenever German teams play in Europe, the choice of attending player is always based on their background or anything else that might connect them to the opposition team. At Arsenal, things were completely different. They didn't want everything to be focused on a single player. Instead, they preferred to send someone who might be less interesting to the media. A single person shouldn't be more important than their team or the game. It made me think. From my experience with the national team, I was used to the fact that the goalscorer was required to attend a presser the day after, but was it really such a good idea to create hype and all sorts of stories around a player who scored a goal during a Champions League group match? After all, things could change completely from one game to the next. Why didn't we allocate the attention more evenly to all players? He didn't need to explain himself, so why didn't we leave the supposed star alone and let his performance speak for itself? The English might be right in their approach. A few days after my move, I found this to be an interesting lesson. Apparently, the German way of doing things didn't have to be the only way. The match in Dortmund ended 1-1. We were in the lead for a long time after a Van Persie goal, but Ivan Perišić equalised just before the final whistle. It was the conclusion to an extreme week, during which I was carrying around a dictionary and trying to find my bearings in a new life.

Ulrike eventually came to London to find us a new house, which the club helped us with. While I was involved in the final decision-making, I didn't make my own wishes a priority. It was more important that my wife and child were happy. If your family is well, you feel all the better for it. It made me play better, too. My first month in London was a great September, warm and bright; the city looked beautiful in the sunshine. October was dry, too. In the beginning, we were surprised how nice the weather was: no worse than in Hannover or Bremen and definitely better than London's reputation suggests.

A few months later, however, we were introduced to the peculiarities of British architecture. Our little red-brick house in Hampstead Garden Suburb was a listed building with rickety windows that wouldn't close properly. It was draughty, the wind blew through every crack, and the roof was leaking. Rainstorms resulted in water dripping from the ceiling, and every now and then, a pipe would burst. Poor Paul, who was barely six months old, was constantly ill. I was on the road with the team a lot and didn't bear the brunt of it, but it was a difficult time for Ulrike.

The decision to move to London meant the inevitable end of her career, and we were aware of that. At thirteen, she had been sent to a Leipzig boarding school specialising in handball. It had become her raison d'être, and now, all of a sudden, it was over. The English aren't into handball, so for her as a competitive athlete, going back to zero was very difficult. Fortunately, in the lead-up to the 2012 Olympics, a handball trend developed that resulted in the formation of a local women's team. Ulrike made friends with a group of Scandinavian students who played in a small league. It was very good for her self-confidence, because while this had nothing to do with professional sport anymore, she could at least continue doing what she loved. It stays with you, this ambition to win and do your best. You can't get rid of it, just like the urge to move, to push yourself physically. She couldn't just sit at home or take the pushchair for a stroll through Hampstead Heath; it would've probably driven her mad. She was desperate for some balance, and I could relate, but it was still an entirely new life for her. Living in a house we couldn't warm to (in every sense), with a newborn baby, in an enormous and fairly anonymous city: the overall experience came as quite a shock. We had to manage that challenge together.

In the beginning, we slightly underestimated the city's size as well as the time and energy we had to invest in it. It took thirty to forty minutes to get from our house to the training ground, and if you were unlucky, there would be an hour's worth of traffic. Getting from A to B in a constantly overcrowded and hectic London was such a hassle that we tended to stay exclusively within our own borough, travelling by foot whenever possible.

When relatives and acquaintances came to visit us, we felt obligated to work through the entire sightseeing programme: Big Ben, Westminster, the Crown Jewels, the London Eye, Madame Tussauds, Tower Bridge — by the time we had finished, we would be exhausted and ready for bed. While footballers enjoy a relatively large amount of free time, acting as a tour guide on the side wasn't going to be compatible with the job in the long run. Our day-to-day life was too taxing for us to be a regular part of the hubbub. As a result, we ended up providing our guests with topped-up Oyster cards, maps, and good tips, and stayed home while they fought their way through hordes of tourists. We might have had an active social life, but we didn't spend much time with my colleagues. New contacts weren't necessarily established in football but rather from playgroup or baby swimming.

We were fortunate to have close friends in Nadine and Richard Baum, who always stood by us and helped with everything. They were both part of this adventure and a genuine part of our little family. The idea to take them to London with us had occurred to me towards the end of the 2010/11 season, when a transfer to Arsenal had first been looming. Jérôme Boateng, who had been at Manchester City at the time, had told me that medical care in England wasn't optimal, which is why it was imperative for me to take my own therapist with me, and I wanted to give it a try in Bremen. Nadine had worked as a physio for Ulrike's handball team, but she was also her best friend: they had lived together in Leipzig.

Nadine's husband was a specialist PE teacher and had played football for Sachsen Leipzig. Because the four of us got along

Being a professional footballer wasn't the be all and end all for me growing up, but I had dreams like any other child. Here I am at a young age kitted out in a sweater based on Germany's iconic 1990 World Cup kit. *[Author's personal collection]*

The TSV Pattensen youth team, 1992. I joined at the age of four and my dad was manager. While he would get irate on the sidelines, I was placid on the field. We developed into quite the side, later becoming regional champions. *[Author's personal collection]*

My first Hannover 96 player pass. When I joined the club at a young age I had no great expectations of making the grade, but I turned out to be a late developer and ended up leapfrogging players that had once seemed so much better than me.
[Author's personal collection]

With my teammates from the Lower Saxony county side at the Under-20 National Cup in Duisburg, 2003. Getting the call up to represent your region is a big deal. *[Author's personal collection]*

Bob Marley's music was the soundtrack to our lives as kids and my bedroom walls were decorated with a giant Jamaica flag and a picture of his face. *[Colorsport/Imago]*

One of the players I found it particularly difficult against in my early days was Schalke 04's Ebbe Sand. He was a master of movement and it was impossible to keep up with him. Here I am putting the ball into my own net with him lurking on my shoulder in March 2004. *[Getty]*

Borussia Dortmund's Jan Koller was a far more ominous presence than Sand, but rather more straightforward to deal with. I won the battle of the giants during this game, stealing a march on the Czech to earn Hannover a 1-1 draw in injury time. *[Getty]*

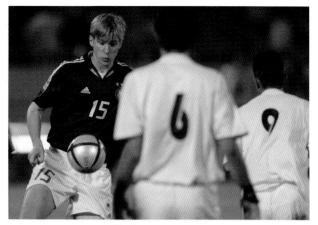

Despite my obvious lack of experience, I was called up to the national team in October 2004 by Jürgen Klinsmann, making my debut as a substitute two weeks after my twentieth birthday in a 2-1 win over Iran in Tehran. *[Getty]*

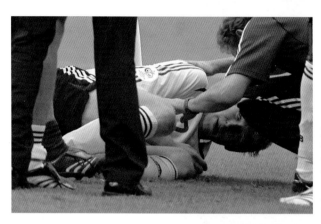

Klinsmann's vision allowed us youngsters to develop as internationals ahead of the 2006 World Cup on home soil. Following our victory in the quarter-final shootout over Argentina, I took a kick to the private region from an annoyed Leandro Cufré, sparking a brawl. *[Offside]*

We had an excellent tournament under Klinsmann, only to agonisingly miss out in extra time of our semi-final against Italy in Dortmund. *[Getty]*

Following a successful World Cup, I made the move to Werder Bremen, who were a force to be reckoned with at the Weser Stadium. In November 2006 I got the only goal of the game in a 1-0 win in the Champions League over Chelsea. *[Offside]*

Clemens Fritz was one of my closest friends at Bremen and my roommate of five years. After my move to London I kept in touch with him, and today we are business partners, running a property company together. *[Offside]*

Bremen is not a particularly huge city, and we enjoyed a particularly close relationship with the fans, especially on nights like these, when we defeated Real Madrid 3-2 in November 2007. *[Getty]*

On the final day of the 2007/08 season, we needed to win away to Bayer Leverkusen to qualify for the Champions League and did so courtesy of a Markus Rosenberg goal ten minutes before full-time. At full time me and Torsten Frings savoured the moment. *[Getty]*

By 2008 Cristiano Ronaldo was one of the world's best, but he couldn't get on the scoresheet during our 3-2 quarter-final win at Euro 2008. We would lose 1-0 in the final to Spain. *[Offside]*

I wasn't able to take part in the second leg of our UEFA Cup semi-final in 2008 against Hamburg but my teammates, including Naldo, Frank Baumann, Frings, Claudio Pizarro, Sebastian Prödl and Pieter Niemeyer, made sure I was involved in celebrations. We went on to lose the final but won the German Cup. *[Getty]*

Our 4-1 win over England at the 2010 World Cup was controversial due to Frank Lampard's ghost goal, but that didn't matter too much to us. Unfortunately, we couldn't make it to the final, undone by Spain again. *[Offside]*

At the end of August 2011 my move to Arsenal was finally confirmed. Just a couple of weeks before that, I got to face the legendary Michael Ballack for the last time in the Bundesliga, who by this point had rejoined Leverkusen. [*Getty*]

Welcome to the Premier League: I quickly had to get used to the physical and fast nature of the English game. My first game, which came just after Arsenal's 8-2 loss to Manchester United, was a 1-0 win over Swansea. [*Offside*]

Living in London can occasionally present its challenges, but I have grown to love England's capital. *[Offside]*

When I first arrived at Arsenal Wenger was the only man in the dressing room who could speak German, but I was soon joined by my good friend Lukas Podolski, a lively character in the dressing room. *[Offside]*

We were also joined by Mesut Özil from Real Madrid. Wenger gave Özil freedom to inspire the team with creative ideas, though I did occasionally have to remind him of his responsibilities to his teammates, and more importantly the fans… *[Offside]*

With Jürgen Klinsmann following our 1-0 group stage victory over the USA at the 2014 World Cup. Jürgen acted as a mentor to me and so many other young German players in the lead up to the 2014 World Cup, putting a lot of faith in us. *[Offside]*

Consoling my Arsenal teammate Laurent Koscielny following a quarter-final win over France in Rio. The game was played in searing heat and everyone was dead on their feet by full time. *[Offside]*

After years of near misses, 2014 was finally the tournament when our generation went all the way and emulated so many of our predecessors. You can see what it meant to me at the celebrations back home. *[Offside]*

Heading home during the 4-0 win over Aston Villa in the 2015 FA Cup final, by far the most comfortable of the three finals I was involved in with Arsenal. *[Offside]*

In the 2017 final, we were given little hope by the press. My job was to deal with Diego Costa, once described by German newspaper *Süddeutsche Zeitung* as a 'toxic irritant in shorts'. I did my job, and therefore completed a hat-trick of FA Cup titles with Arsenal. *[Offside]*

Draped in the BFG flag as I walk around the Emirates as a player for the last in May 2018, following a 5-0 win over Burnley. [Offside]

very well, Ulrike and I asked them if they could imagine working as my personal, 24/7 support staff, and they thought it was
an exciting idea. We came to a quick financial agreement, and
in the spring of 2011, with the prospect of moving to London
soon, they joined us in our Bremen flat with their little daughter, Charlotta. The set-up was designed for a move to England,
but I would have also employed them for the remaining year
of my contract with Bremen had the transfer not taken place. I
wanted professional support, unattached to the club, because I
noticed that the strain was getting worse; I needed more specialised, more individual care.

At the club, you're one of 25 players, and the physios only
have two hands each. I had learned and benefitted from external
treatment; and so I wanted to build a team that would advance
and improve me. Nadine and Richard were virtually on standby
for all activities. If I wanted, I could have Nadine treat me for
ninety minutes a day or work through extra training sessions
with Richard. Everything happened in secret; Bremen knew
nothing about it. I realised quickly that the system worked. Nadine is a superb therapist. Every day she was an enormous help
to me. Her and Richard have a naturally positive attitude and
a great energy. For an athlete, people like this are invaluable,
especially if you're in a new city by yourself. Arsenal helped us in
our search for two of everything: accommodation, child mind-
ers, you name it. There were bureaucratic obstacles to overcome,
too, but we definitely wanted things to work out. I was aware
that I could only achieve sporting success if I was fit, extremely
well prepared, and armed with the reassurance that if the worst

came to the worst, good people would have my back. It didn't stop with Nadine and Richard, either: I commissioned her to explore the world of sports medicine, because I wanted to bring in external people to cover whatever a physiotherapist and fitness coach couldn't offer me.

Nadine, for instance, never said she knew how to do everything. Instead, she would send me to other therapists, who might know more about certain specialised subjects. Again and again, we flew in osteopaths and kinesiologists from Spain and Berlin to try out different tricks. Flights, hotels, and fees would amount to four-figure sums for every three-day stay. I also wanted both Nadine and Richard to make progress themselves, so they took courses in new techniques. Nadine learned to apply Liebscher-Bracht's pain therapy, a form of treatment that operates with specific movement exercises and selective pressure on muscles and tendons. Another tool for the physios' toolbox. We were our own miniature clinic: an experimental laboratory always on the lookout for effective methods, with the primary goal of performing on the pitch. Nadine attended to me after every training. I would drive from London Colney straight to their house, where they treated me for up to two hours a day: either for prophylaxis or with a specific target, most often the heel or the knee. Liebscher-Bracht, acupuncture, foot baths, Kinesio tape; Nadine knew them all, but our main concern was releasing tensions, correcting bad positioning, and checking my pelvic posture: was it straight, was I able to move well? If not, Nadine would reset it.

These one, two hours of extra treatment made a huge difference. Richard and I did do some fitness work but compared to what I used to do at Bremen, that started to take a back seat over time. It couldn't be done to that extent anymore, anyway. Instead, I found other ways to get rid of pain and become healthier in general. Nadine and Richard are excellent cooks, and over the years, they've acquired a lot of nutritional knowledge. I wanted their input: what did I need, what would help me, how could I improve a little bit every day? We changed things up a lot, with soy products, coconut yoghurt, fruit and linseed oils, nuts, and less meat. Before I ate the breakfast he prepared for me, Richard would often come over early in the morning to supervise my stretching exercises or drills designed to activate certain parts of the brain. You're more focused when there's someone looking over your shoulder. I invested a lot into my fitness, in every sense of the word. My personal network cost me several hundred thousand euros a year, ten percent of my net salary. But it was the right decision to make, especially because it paid off: I ended up extending my four-year contract by another three seasons. Without these additional therapies, I could have never played seven years at a top Premier League club.

Experience has taught me that you can't possibly do enough towards your physical health. For example, I've always been a fan of yoga. I was introduced to it when I first joined the national team and soon noticed that it could give me stability and flexibility. At 33, I was one of the most flexible players at Arsenal and would shake my head in disbelief at how tight and closed some colleagues' locomotor systems were. Apart from me, barely anyone attended the yoga sessions offered by the club. There would

usually be four us: Héctor Bellerín, Nacho Monreal, Tomáš Rosický, and myself. It was a crash course but on a medium level: a
bit of stretching, a couple of positions, a bit of stability training.
An hour of tensing and relaxing, as opposed to the kind of yoga
practiced at the DFB. Most of the Arsenal squad would sneer at
these exercises. They thought we were meditating. 'There's no
ball anywhere, this is so uncool.' They were only happy with a
ball at their feet, so there was no incentive to do it. 'I'm turning
up to training and that's enough.'

Except it isn't, not if you want to sustain a certain level or
step up your performance. It was difficult to convey the concept: either you learn to take personal responsibility from the
beginning, from parents, teachers, and coaches around you, or
you never do. We need to counteract this kind of narrow-mind-
edness. In autumn 2017, an Under-18s player approached me to
ask if we could sit down for a chat. I nearly keeled over in shock:
six and a half years I had been with the club, and something like
that had never happened before. He wanted to talk to me about
leadership; maybe his coach had been pushing him. It took a lot
of energy to convince my teammates to do more for their bodies, to take a look at some things the club offered and try them
out. Unfortunately, in the long run, barely anyone was willing to
work purposefully on their weaknesses.

The first few matches with Arsenal went fairly well. During
the 2-1 win at Norwich City, however, I was simply pushed out
of the way and didn't know what was going on before the ball
hit the back of our net. I should have got to the ball sooner. In
Germany, I might have had more time in this situation or the

chance to position my body in the right place, but that didn't work in the Premier League. Technically, the standard was comparable with the Bundesliga, but the higher pace forced you to recalculate many of the distances you thought you knew. Many opposing players were either enormously fast — real sprinters — or proper units, built like decathletes, with an incredible physique. You couldn't just push them away in the air. In addition, English referees tend to ignore more incidents. You might think a foul was committed, but they'll just allow play to continue. I had several of these moments. I had to adapt my way of playing to the local conventions.

Many a time, I also had to thank Robin van Persie privately: he played an outstanding season, and some of his 37 goals bailed me out after some less-than-successful moments. Corners and free-kicks against us were extremely stressful. Because we were rather short as a team, we generally wanted to avoid opposition set-pieces. I might have stood at the back as a tall centre-half, but around me, there would usually be at least two forwards and two defenders who were the size of wardrobes. The physical power that faced you in the Premier League was brutal. On the ground, we were superior to most teams, so many of them switched to long balls, hunting for the knock-downs and the second ball. That approach could be dramatic, especially during away games. At the Emirates, on our own turf, we could do our own thing. Many of the smaller teams would come to London already anticipating that they would walk away empty-handed. But away from home, it was a different story. Pokey grounds, lots of wind — it was far more difficult to play with our sleek style there, and too often we didn't manage to do so. There were dressing rooms not much bigger than a phone booth, where you would virtually sit on top of each other. Every small-town ground in the German hinterland was equipped more luxuriously. The interior designer responsible for the dressing rooms at QPR had a particularly special idea: in the middle of the room stood a toilet, with a door that had neither a top nor a bottom. I can't imagine this being allowed in Germany, but it did have a certain charm. It amused me. When you enter a room like that, you know exactly what the day's going to be like and what awaits you on the pitch. You could tell there was work to be done and challenges to be faced. Forget love, peace, and harmony: here, they were going to batter you from the start, and the crowd were going to be roaring from the stands. Away from home, the boos were even stronger than in Germany, but occasionally, the home fans would see you off with applause after a particularly good performance. The tighter things were in tin cans like Loftus Road and the worse the smell, the more you would come together as a team and the closer you would return to the roots of the game. With the exception of one or two modern stadiums like the Emirates or the Etihad, away team dressing rooms were purposely designed to be uncomfortable. There were two shower heads for 25 people, they generally ejected boiling hot water, and you had to take care not to get up off the wooden benches with a splinter in your backside. All this was designed to intimidate the better teams, but interestingly, the effect was often the exact opposite. Those stuffy broom cupboards made you move closer together, both literally and figuratively: there was more conversation than in our own spacious, spotless stadium. For me personally, the bigger problem during away games came with the low ceilings in rooms and corridors; I had to crouch to be able to stand and walk. Over the years, I bumped my head so many times that a horn almost grew on my forehead, a permanent lump. I hit everything: a monitor on the bus, door frames, you name it. Perhaps I should have got myself a protective helmet like Petr Čech.

Following my Norwich blunder, I allowed myself to be out-smarted a few more times, and the papers' reaction was scathing. The *Daily Mail* described me of having 'all the grace of broken deckchair', and the *Daily Mirror* said my mobility reminded them of the recently unveiled statues of Tony Adams, Herbert Chapman, and Thierry Henry. I didn't read those reviews. In Hannover, I had grown up with the local papers, and as a pro-fessional, I would occasionally take a look to see the ratings. In London, however, I knew none of the papers, so I didn't visit the newsagents to buy any. Arsenal forbids newspapers in the dress-ing room, which meant I didn't notice headlines or bad reviews. Keeping it all at arm's length helped me keep my cool. Things became unpleasant, though, whenever German papers or news agencies would copy these lines word-for-word without having seen the match or accounting for the character of English tab-loids. In German, everything sounded even harsher than it was intended to, which became a burden to me.

This is making the rounds in Germany, and everyone's reading it, including Jogi Löw, I thought. *Everyone's going to think I'm totally rubbish in England.*

It was stressful. In his anger over their coverage, my father cancelled his *Kicker* subscription. During a phase like this, you need a lenient manager like Wenger, who'll tell you, 'Yes, you make mistakes, but you're intelligent enough to learn your lessons from them. I'm sure you'll cut them out. I don't doubt that, and I don't doubt you. You're going to be important to the team.'

I was able to talk openly to him about my problems and ask him a lot of questions. He was patient with me and didn't allow himself to be influenced by outside opinions. Another coach would probably have dropped me to protect himself. Arsenal's programme described my initial difficulties in a reserved manner typical of the British: 'Of all the new signings, his learning curve was the steepest.' In those weeks, I had to learn the hard way, but thanks to Wenger's unwavering trust, it was allowed to be a long learning curve. By Christmas, I had adapted fairly well to the game's pace and toughness. The Arsenal fans had begun to honour my style of play in their special way, chanting 'Big fucking German, we have a big fucking German,' to the tune of 'Guantanamera'. I didn't know what to think of it at first, until my colleagues explained that it was meant as a sign of affection: the crowd were pleased to have such a bloody tall bloke on their team who took care of things at the back with German efficiency.

I did notice, though, how hard it was to get through a season without a winter break. You're on duty continuously from August to late May, and you can't imagine how tiring that is, especially for the mind. *Four more weeks of pulling myself together*, I would think when my energy reserves used to approach zero in Germany around November. *Four more weeks and I'll be free to recover*. The prospect of a two-week holiday, of Christmas and

New Year with the family, helped me through that gloomy time. You get to November in England and they tell you that in another four weeks, things are taking off properly, with games every three days and everything cranked up to another level of intensity. It's not very uplifting. The days get so short that afternoons feel like evenings. Everything is grey, even your insides; you're in a relegation battle against yourself. In early January, I virtually collapsed. I spent three days in bed in my cold house. I wasn't sure what exactly was wrong with me, but I had evidently crossed a line. I trudged through games, far from my best and in a frail mental state. Was I out of place here after all? Would Löw let me start at the Euros if I wasn't convincing at Arsenal?

It was too much for me; my body was screaming for a break. And it would get it. Following a header during a fixture against Sunderland, I had a funny feeling after the landing. Something had cracked on the inside of my right ankle. I thought I would keep playing and run off the pain, but then I accelerated to a sprint and it was agony. It felt as if I'd been shot. Because the tibia was slightly broken, the entire ligament structure had come loose. The ligaments were exposed and had ruptured completely at the next opportunity. There was my break – three months. It was my worst professional injury to date, just before the Euros, too. The diagnosis was staggering: another surgery despite all the work and slog. Just like every other year.

Was that normal? Under normal conditions, had my power and energy been at top level, nothing would have happened in such a harmless situation. But when your mind and muscles are exhausted, there's danger in every step. Controls and balances stop working, and parts of the body slip off in the wrong direction, like train compartments derailing.

Trying to be fit for the tournament was a race against time. Realistically, my chances were minimal. During rehab at Donaustauf, Daniel Delonga, my consultant at Adidas at the time, advised me to work with Lars Lienhard. Lars was a former track athlete, sports scientist, and pioneer of the neural-controlled training method. The basic idea being that athletes are only as strong as their weakest part, because the human locomotor system is interconnected, interdependent, and controlled by the brain and the nervous system. I was always open to new forms of therapy, so I met with him away from the rehab clinic, wanting to avoid potential conflict: physiotherapists often operate with different opinions and approaches that might clash with each other. Teachings tend to collide, but that mustn't discourage you. To me, additional stimuli were always very important. I did what benefited me, even if it hadn't been agreed upon or might seem counterproductive. Muscles are like soldiers, Lars explained: they only perform tasks ordered by the brain, without you noticing. At the same time, muscles, tendons, and joints send information back to the brain. If one or both sides don't provide enough information — if there are issues with understanding, for example, or the nerves are damaged from an injury — the locomotor system won't run smoothly. After my many surgeries, the drive of certain muscle groups had virtually disappeared. Every procedure inflicts damage on the body; every scar interrupts signal transmission. Imagine it like a blind spot, a dead zone. Your brain says, 'I know nothing about that spot.

There might be danger ahead.' As a result, the command is executed in a reluctant, uncontrolled, and sloppy manner, which in turn produces problems elsewhere. You find yourself running from one surgery to the next, and your body no longer knows what the hell is going on.

In my case, my restricted mobility impinged on my knees and joints. Lars had me do very distinct, focused exercises in order to free the blocked paths in my nervous system. Working with him brought on incredible success: I was shocked by the results. We always assume that as long we can run and see properly, everything is fine – just as long nothing hurts. But that's a mistake. Lars showed me how great a factor the eyes are — in everything we do, but especially when it comes to timing. My timing was great on the right, but when the ball came from the other side, I got the feeling my left eye didn't really want to know. Why was that? How could I train myself so I wouldn't have to turn my head to look to the left? Why was my visual perception stronger in my right eye? How many times was the ball coming from my left when I was playing centre-half? At least half of the time, and in fifty percent of those situations, my brain would say, 'Listen, I can't quite see the ball there, so I'd rather not jump.' And because my left eye didn't really want to look at the ball either, I kept craning my neck in order to use my right, dominant one to compensate.

Football spends little to no time on these things, even though they could be crucial. People prefer weights and isolated exercises with dumbbells. But what good was that to me on the pitch? What really was the benefit to the movements required during a match? These kinds of concerns are barely addressed anymore. Before the 2006 World Cup, Jürgen Klinsmann hired American specialists for stability exercises, and while those are still practiced today, the concept is outdated already. What was the next step? How could the body be prepared for burdens in a specific and individual way? While there is always talk of activating the body before training, be it with some stretching exercises or something similar, that only focusses on literal mechanics. Shouldn't you also perform some eye exercises to make you feel better, to make your torso more flexible, and to ensure that your hands can reach closer to the floor? It's an interesting approach.

The exercises with Lars showed clearly how differently both my eyes would move when simple objects came towards me. Instead of focussing on the object, my left eye would always stay in the centre, so Lars showed me a way to increase its activity. I put an eye patch over my right eye to force the left one to focus. After a few weeks, I actually noticed a difference during games. My feeling for a high ball coming from the left had improved a lot, as had my timing with headers. My eye was confident, which meant my head no longer needed to twist and turn. Whenever your cervical spine is required to turn, danger is always imminent. The better your standing and the straighter your spine, especially around the neck area, the better and faster your performance. Lars kept telling me to look at Cristiano Ronaldo: 'When he runs, it looks like there's a rod in his back. Now you know why he's so fast.'

My body reacted brilliantly to the training. We did before-and-after tests to see which drills I benefitted from and which ones put too much strain on my eyes. There were exercises that granted me more control over my knees; the steering had improved, too, even in my weakened ankle. It was all coming back. After rehab, Lars would fly to London every five weeks so we could do prophylactic work. With his help, I stayed fit for four and a half years, broke through the vicious circle of injury-rehab-injury, and had my best years athletically. Meeting Lars had changed my life in football. The trick was not to rely only on those periodic exercises with Lars but to calibrate yourself before games — like with push-ups for the eyes: you take a pen and move it towards your head, and your eyes will move to the centre. Whenever I did it at training, many wondered if I had lost my mind, but I ignored them. Most of the time, I did my exercises at home or in hotel rooms before games with a video of six, seven six, seven exercises. Sometimes, I would do them in the dressing room just before kick-off. I couldn't care less about the reactions from others: in my late twenties, I was at an advanced age and so took the liberty to do strange things. It didn't matter if someone laughed. It was an example, though, of how anything new and unknown was met with laughter rather than intrigue. For me personally, the football business has always lacked curiosity. Arsène Wenger let me be; he trusted his players. Over the years, Arsenal expanded their range: a number of physios joined the team as well as a yoga instructor, an osteopath, and a few psychologists. Whoever wanted to draw on these options was free to do so, but the focus remained on massages and classical physiotherapy, and rightly so. What I was doing with Lars introduced two to three factors to the game that I hadn't encountered in football until then. I kept the ratios healthy, though, because you still had to accept and apply the processes prescribed by the club.

At my suggestion, Lars was taken along to Brazil for the 2014 World Cup, where five or six players would work with him at a facility close to our quarters. Benedikt Höwedes, who during the tournament played left-back for the first time in his career, was prepared by Lars for the new point of view which came with the position. Mario Götze and Jérôme Boateng also joined the group. But the set-up was far from ideal. Lars's methods were new and different, and the DFB physios were concerned that his exercises wouldn't agree with their own specific measures. At the moment, football isn't ready for a paradigm shift, to move away from working on the odd ailment and towards a holistic treatment of the athlete that covers everything: body, mind, and soul. Psychological factors in particular are being neglected heavily when, in reality, they're of equal relevance. Many parts of your life have an effect on your subconscious, slowly eating you alive. It could be a divorce from fifteen years ago or being furious with a friend or family member. There are so many things that trouble you, both knowingly and otherwise, and which rob you of your energy. Your body stores it all, until one day, you get your comeuppance. Your body is your mind's only chance to draw attention to itself. What effect, for instance, might it have on training the next day or on your next injury? Quite apart from that, is it a good idea for an athlete to have a tattoo done, which really just means injecting ink into your own body? Probably not.

At the moment, neither football nor footballers are ready to ask these questions, let alone answer them. Doing so would take both time and money. Unfortunately, footballers are used to working a mere three hours a day, while other athletes devote themselves to their profession all day long. We have all the money in the world, but we can't seem to realise just how important our bodies are. On average, you get seven years of playing professionally, ten to fifteen if things go perfectly. Shouldn't you be compelled to do anything you can to make the most of that time? Many don't even know what the maximum is. They're more concerned with having fun on the pitch, but there is more to being a professional than that. Our industry is narrow-minded; you hang on to the methods you're familiar with. For a while, Werder Bremen employed an energetics consultant called Kurt Schweinberger, who worked with special liquids and sound waves. We would put on headsets and listen to rushing sounds. On match days, we would do it lying down. He had a different programme and massage oil for each injury. Half the squad went along with the whole thing while the others refused, calling it 'mumbo jumbo'. I saw it through to the end in order to see the effects for myself, and it helped me immensely.

Opening myself up to new influences and developing an appetite for new people and new ideas has always been a very important experience for me. For every interesting approach introduced to us, though, there was always at least one person who'd say, 'That's bollocks, what's the point?' Reactions like this used to ring alarm bells in my mind: now, I wanted to try it all the more. There are so many exciting things in sports medicine that could be interesting to people in football over the years. Clubs are going to have to change the way they think; they'll have to reposition themselves for financial reasons alone. If your squad costs you £200m a year and a quarter of them are sidelined due to injury, £50m is being wasted. These are incredible sums, so what could make more sense than realigning your priorities accordingly and doing all you can for the health of your players?

Over the years, the cooperation between Lars and I grew. I stuck with the training, even when doubts would arise or when I couldn't really be bothered to exert my brain. It's the kind of work that annoys you initially, because it targets your nerves. The key was to stick with it consistently and feel the effect. There's no point in trying it once, only to dismiss it. That was the mistake some teammates made. I saw the programme through over the years and am living proof that it works. Lars, Nadine, Richard, and everyone else in my set-up helped me take the final ten to fifteen percent onto the pitch with me. I'm not the kind of person who finishes their career and says, 'That was a great experience. It furthered me but probably won't help anyone else.'

There is the idea of maintaining the network I built up in London, so that others might benefit from it. In my new life as manager of Arsenal Academy, I do everything in my power to inspire young players. So far, I have lived to see a lot, especially with regards to health and fitness: I want to challenge people to explore ideas, but more importantly, I want to protect them as well as I can from injuries to mind and body. I want to convince them that they need to put in the work if they want to be world class, and I want to set an example for them. For me, there wasn't a well-defined route to the very top, but I still made it in the end, because I did everything I could to give myself the best chance possible. Talent is what you make of it.

After rehab, I returned to London for the last three weeks of the season but wasn't called into action. It was clear to Wenger that I wasn't going to be match-fit in time, and he let me join up with the national team ahead of schedule. 'Have yourself checked,' he said. 'See whether or not you're ready to go to the Euros. We'll be back on the attack next season.' Arsenal won 3-2 at West Brom in the final game of the season, which meant we would finish fourth and had again qualified for the Champions League. Getting into Europe was crucial for the club who, despite being owned by Stan Kroenke, funds itself. Accordingly, contracts were designed on a performance-related basis: reaching the Champions League earned you a bonus of ten to twenty percent of your annual income. Overall, that will have been anywhere between twenty and thirty million pounds for the whole squad.

I ended up going to the Euros but didn't play a single match: Löw's decision meant I had to yield my spot to someone else. It annoyed me deeply, but at the same time it motivated me for the next season. For pre-season, I would, in Wenger's words, be back on the attack. I was no longer first choice for the national team, and the long-term injury had removed me temporarily from the picture at Arsenal, too. I wouldn't stand for it. Ultimately, though, despite the disappointment, not being deployed during the tournament had been a blessing in disguise: I'm not sure that my ankle could have withstood the strain after such a short time. We'll never know, but my gut tells me it wouldn't have gone well. I felt different than I had done after my three previous international tournaments. Following the World Cups in Germany and South Africa as well as the Euros in Austria and Switzerland, I had returned either injured or completely drained and susceptible to new injuries. In comparison, 2012 saw me go on holiday with my fitness at top level. It was brilliant; I was able to resume training straight away and begin the year from a position of strength.

In the meantime, we had moved. The new house was only five minutes from the old one but much more modern, and with double glazing. The rain no longer found its way into our living room, the wind no longer blew the cold through the corridors, and there was no more flooding. We were considerably more comfortable and felt much more at home. Moving house twice with a toddler in the space of a few months hadn't exactly been pleasant, but at least it had given us the opportunity to have a clear-out. When you move frequently, the important things inevitably fall by the wayside; you only take the bare necessities.

I had a new German teammate and neighbour in Lukas Podolski. He lived just around the corner, so we carpooled to training. Fortunately for me, Poldi was quite liberal when it came to the stereo and didn't insist on playing Die Höhner on loop. Before the beginning of the season, the two of us, together with Bacary Sagna, flew to Nigeria for a sponsor's event. The private plane landed in Mallorca to refuel before continuing to Lagos. I had never made a trip abroad just for promotional purposes before. In Lagos, there were yellow buses driving around everywhere, and our hotel suffered the occasional power cut. What's going on here? Our mission was to do a dance on an event stage after studying the choreography. Safe to say we set the place on fire. Later, there was a fan festival, attended by five hundred people, and we danced again. People were loving it.

For the first time, I felt the power Arsenal had overseas. I could not have imagined anything like it. It was good to have Poldi by my side. He has a positive outlook on everything and doesn't take himself too seriously; he was just the right person for a trip like this. A year later, during an Asia tour, we stood on a podium dressed as Samurai warriors, bashing each other with swords. It was just nice to have someone like that on the team, someone who enjoyed life both as a footballer and life in general every day, unrelated to the weather. It helped me, too. Throughout his three years at Arsenal, he scored some sensational goals with that hammer of a left foot, and as a result of our time at the club, we also managed to work well together on the national team.

During my first year in London, I was virtually on my own when it came to languages. Thanks to his time at Dortmund, I was able to exchange at least a few words with Tomáš Rosický, while Robin van Persie didn't get beyond bratwurst. But the situation gave me the opportunity to work on my rudimentary English. When Poldi and Mesut Özil arrived as well, we would have conversations with each other and crack the occasional German joke, which helped all three of us to cope. At a team like Arsenal, where foreigners outnumber the English, small groups tend to form automatically. Some will speak French, the other Spanish. From 2013, we built our own little German gang. We had a good time together. Poldi's English was good; he had a real gift for languages and didn't struggle to acclimatise at all. Mesut's was actually very good too: it tended not to show, but he could if he wanted.

Because we supported each other, many things that to me had been new and complicated, like registering with the council, went without a hitch for the other two. Together with centre-foward Olivier Giroud, Poldi had joined the club as replacement for Van Persie, who after being voted Player of the Year had left for Manchester United before the beginning of the season. It was to be Sir Alex Ferguson's last campaign, during which Van Persie's goals won the league for his new club. He had been the captain and a real superstar at Arsenal, so the Dutchman left behind a vacuum. The team may not have been falling apart, but we did need a new leader. Thomas Vermaelen came out on top, which, speaking from an egoistic standpoint, wasn't good news for me, because it meant that Thomas was guaranteed to start. I now had to fight Laurent Koscielny for the other central defender's position.

Unfortunately, at Arsenal, it was commonplace to sell many good players. Renovating the new stadium, which had been completed in 2006, had cost a lot of money, so those in charge took a cautious approach to financing. It was bad luck that the move from Highbury to the Emirates happened at the same time as the appearance of powerful investors elsewhere, like oligarch Roman Abramovich at Chelsea and Sheikh Mansour at Manchester City, for whom money was virtually no object. The club hadn't won a trophy since the 2005 FA Cup final and was now falling behind. Still, our team was good enough to compete for the championship every year. Defensively, 2012/13 was Arsenal's best start to a season since 1934, as we kept clean three sheets in our opening three league games. I started all three of those matches and so didn't give Wenger the opportunity to keep me stewing on the bench, and I featured in all but four of Arsenal's league matches during that campaign.

My absolute highlight of the season came in November, during the North London derby. Typically, days before that fixture, something seems to loom over both boroughs. The air carries a specific mood, a kind of electrical tension. A storm is coming, and if things go badly, it's going to blow you away. No, it's not a regular match, not by far. In the stadium, the difference is instantly noticeable. Usually, the Emirates crowd, spoiled by various title wins and aesthetically high-quality football, were fairly quiet during run-of-the-mill games and even took their time warming up in the Champions League. But when it came to Tottenham, they got down to business immediately, celebrating every throw-in. On the pitch, everyone knew they had to do even more, which may sound odd because professionals always aspire to give a hundred percent anyway, but combined with the emotions in the stands, you still end up adding another ten percent. It was the weight of the derby.

Tottenham took the lead after ten minutes: we had been trying for an offside trap but only with three of our back four, and ex-Gunner Emmanuel Adebayor tapped in after Jermain Defoe had broken through. Seven minutes later, Adebayor was sent off after a brutal sliding tackle against Santi Cazorla. The game changed. After Tottenham cleared a set piece, Theo Walcott won the ball, sprinted past his opponent along the touchline and put in a beautiful, out-swinging cross that spun away from the 'keeper. I was positioned just right, beyond the back of the defender, and soared into the air, thundering a header into the top corner. My first goal in England, my first goal for Arsenal. Against Tottenham, too, of all teams. Sharing this feeling with the fans was a wonderful experience, and it's hard to describe. There is no greater satisfaction than seeing tens of thousands of people explode with joy at the same time. In the end, we won 5-2, a little piece of history, and a small step towards giving something back to the club I had followed as a child. I was beside myself with pride.

Regrettably, we allowed ourselves a phase of weakness at the turn of the year. We were eliminated from the FA Cup, lost ground in our pursuit of fourth place in the table and our chances of reaching the Champions League quarter-finals were next-to-zero after a 3-1 loss to Bayern during the first leg of the round of sixteen. Munich had got us all flustered at the Emirates with their razor-sharp pressing, and to make matters worse, we lost 2-1 to Spurs in the league two weeks later. We were only fifth in the league, seven points behind Tottenham, whose supporters were already celebrating a shift in power.

Wenger reacted. Koscielny replaced Vermaelen as the second centre-half next to me. His agility and speed made the Frenchman a good match. As different types of defender, we complemented each other well. The new stability at the back helped the team to ten league games without defeat. At the end of a wild race to catch up, we found ourselves in fourth place, a point ahead of Tottenham. Once again, our dear friends had celebrated too soon. We very nearly kicked Bayern out of the Champions

League, too. We won the return leg at the Allianz Arena 2-0; one more goal and Jupp Heynckes' team would have been eliminated. They would go on to win the final 2-1 at Wembley against Borussia Dortmund, securing an historic treble. I benefited indirectly from Bayern's success and the remarkable performance of Jürgen Klopp's Dortmund. German domestic football, which was generally of little interest to anyone in England, had suddenly become top of the world. It made my life at Arsenal easier, especially in the dressing room: the respect shown to German teams had increased, and it was rubbing off on Lukas and me. With their pace and perfect pressing, both Bayern and Dortmund had reached an unprecedented level for Bundesliga teams. Tactically, German clubs were way ahead of the English.

The strong end to the campaign had shown us how much potential our team had. We managed to carry that momentum over into the next season, where, apart from a 3-1 opening day loss to Aston Villa and a tight 1-0 defeat to Man United, we didn't lose a game until December. Across both seasons in 2013, no team in England picked up more points than we did. Mesut played a large part in the upswing. As a gifted footballer, it was easier to find his bearings here than it had been for me. He had a feeling for space and passes which translated to English football, and the others realised how good he was to play with. In next to no time, Mesut became enormously important for us. His success in England was so groundbreaking that the *Guardian* abandoned its editorial guidelines. Then, the house style-guide rule not to capitalise Germanic umlauts was 'no longer tenable', as phrased in an internal email that was later published. 'Özil' was finally allowed to be Özil, and he used the freedoms granted to him by Wenger to inspire his teammates with creative ideas.

In the meantime, I had been made interim captain, because Vermaelen and his deputy Arteta were both injured. It was a great honour and a confirmation, too, that I had finally arrived as a player in England. In autumn 2013, Wenger also indicated that my contract would be extended. The captaincy brought with it duties that I hadn't known about. As captain, you, your counterpart, and the assistant managers had to meet with the match officials for a pre-game conference. The referee would tell you what he wished for, how he was feeling, and that he would welcome it if we supported him. We were supposed to keep in contact with him and prevent officials from being hassled. Some German media referred to me as 'Arsenal's head of defence', but they were wrong. It was one of those phrases outsiders would shout from the rooftops, because they enjoyed labelling people. It also meant they had someone to roast if things didn't go well. Communication was important, of course, but applying that principle to only one person would have been dangerous. Every individual still had to play their part and give commands.

I found it surprising how little conversation took place on the pitch in general. Similar to Germany, everyone seemed to be more concerned with their own performance. We weren't coached in verbal communication, the assumption being that either the 'keeper or the defenders were keeping an eye on everything and taking care of it all. The other teams didn't tend to talk much, either. I can imagine that other sports are much louder. In my opinion, providing assistance to your teammates is crucial and should be fundamental. Coaches need to take more care in teaching their players to communicate. There is a danger that football could become more and more individual. If I'm the one who scored the goal, then I've done my job — a team sport cannot work like this. It was crucial to Wenger that I did a lot of talking during both training and games. One of his favourite words was solidarity. To him, it meant not just looking after yourself on the pitch – you have to keep an eye on the group. Later, I would carry this concept with me to the Academy.

My central defensive partnership with Laurent was very successful. From April 2013 to January 2014, we played 27 full games together: nineteen wins, eight draws, no defeats, and sixteen clean sheets. They were our best, most stable performances. The statistics are a little misleading, because as a team we did lose occasionally, but only if the two of us didn't play over ninety minutes. During the 6-3 defeat to Manchester City just before Christmas 2013, for example, Laurent got injured in the first half. After the final whistle, I got into an argument with Mesut, who was so disappointed by the result that he didn't want to thank the fans. I demanded he come to the stands with me, but he refused. It was the last straw. 'If you wave me off one more time…' I was fuming. 'The Germans will sort it out between themselves,' said Wenger when the press approached him about the incident. And so we did. 'We win and lose together,' Mesut said on social media.

Our flaw was failing to win the big games. We dominated tactically weaker teams, but when equal ones withheld the ball for a longer period of time, we would routinely be knocked out of our stride. When we came up against Bayern again at the Emirates during the round of sixteen in the Champions League, we were clearly the better team — in the beginning, that is, until Mesut missed a penalty and Wojciech Szczęsny was sent off for committing a professional foul. Facing Pep Guardiola's passing machine with ten men was a suicide mission. They tired us out, scored twice, and eliminated us with a one-all draw in the second leg. In the league, meanwhile, we had lost some of our crispness from earlier in the season. In January, we were ousted from the top of the table, and in late March, we lost Wenger's one thousandth Premier League game in a humiliating manner: 6-0 to José Mourinho's Chelsea.

In the run-up to the match, Mourinho had labelled Wenger 'a specialist in failure', which made us feel even more ashamed of our performance. Wenger was the kind of coach who always protected his team in public and bottled everything up privately. He took responsibility for everything, kept pressure away from the squad, and absolutely loathed losing. He dedicated 95 percent of his time to the club, and every great defeat would leave a mark on him. He aged immensely during that time. We empathised with him, but did so even more with our fans, whom, given our potential as a side, we disappointed far too often. Somehow, though, we usually found a way to save the season.

In 2014, we managed to do so with two mad games at Wembley. The FA Cup semi-final saw us play Wigan; we were clear favourites and were already anticipating the final against Hull. However, after half an hour I gave away a penalty and they took the lead. Under Uwe Rösler, they were playing with a back five, which by the standards of the league at the time was highly unusual. We played and played and played, creating chances but without converting them. It was one of those days when you knew early on that nothing would come of it. Eight minutes before the end, though, Alex Oxlade-Chamberlain sent in a cross and, having stayed up front out of desperation, the ball found my head. 1-1. It was just the bit of madness we had needed. A penalty shootout followed. I stood in the centre circle next to Kieran Gibbs; we were peering at Łukasz Fabiański in the distance and both thought we had to help him somehow. 'Send him as much positive energy as you can!' Kieran called. In this moment, we had to believe in something, or rather someone. Him. In my mind, one phrase played on a loop: *You'll save that ball.* I was convinced that our positive energy could bring him to jump to the right corner. He did. Twice. We were through to the final.

Wembley again. Once more, everyone was assuming we wouldn't have any sort of issue against an almost-relegated Hull team. Once more, though, we dealt badly with the situation. After two set pieces in eight minutes, Hull were 2-0 up. We looked at each other, wondering. It was like a nightmare. You wanted to wake up, find that it was still the morning before the final, and that nothing had happened yet. Santi Cazorla soon brought us back into the game, though, finding the top-corner with a free-kick from 25 yards. An amazing moment. Game on. Koscielny's leveller twenty minutes before the end wasn't quite as pretty, but that mattered to no one. Hull's dream was destroyed.

By extra time they were exhausted, and after Olivier Giroud had flicked the ball into his path, Aaron Ramsey scored with the outside of his foot. It was over. There it was, Arsenal's — and Arsène's — first trophy in nine years. The fans had forgotten how it felt. The outburst on the pitch was extreme; the fear of failing against the underdog was unloaded in an unbridled celebration. Everyone was in each other's arms, even hours later during the party at Rosewood London. I could barely process the situation; it was as if it was all happening to someone else. The idea that I was wearing an Arsenal kit and holding the FA Cup in my hands at Wembley was too absurd to be true. The next day, we obeyed that old custom, taking an open-top bus tour through Islington. It led us through areas we don't usually see, like vast council estates. People were standing on balconies and roofs, some had climbed street lamps. The team had ended their long wait for a trophy. We could see the excitement everywhere we went; everyone wanted to enjoy this moment. Thirty, forty thousand people, young, old, and from all walks of life, were united in a peaceful love for the club that had caused them such heartache since 2005. In close proximity to each other in the streets, squad and fans were almost one. As a player, you had earned your right to wear the shirt, and on this Sunday, everything else was insignificant.

It was interesting to see how strongly rooted such a gigantic club still was within its own community. In Germany, new stadiums are built on green grassland or hills on the outskirts of town, and every time that happens, the club in question always loses a piece of its local identity. The Emirates is parked between rows of Victorian dollhouses, like a giant UFO, and is still a stone's throw from the luxury flats built where Highbury used to stand. The club have remained loyal to their neighbourhood despite globalisation, commercialisation, and the investors from oversees. In Germany, you would never find a stadium in the middle of town.

2014 was my best year: the cup win with Arsenal, becoming world champion with Germany, and the birth of our second son. Oscar came into the world in May. Born in London, he is automatically entitled to British citizenship and could play for England one day. We'll see. Originally, Ulrike had wanted him delivered in an NHS hospital. She looked around in Watford, far away from our house. The one she did visit looked like a sickbay; some people were being treated in the corridors, because there weren't enough beds. Ultimately, Ulrike decided on a private hospital. The British healthcare system suffers from a lack of funding. If you don't have private insurance, they make you wait weeks, sometimes months, for doctor's appointments and routine operations. People tolerate this with an admirable stoicism, but I do sometimes think they put up with too much.

After the World Cup in Brazil, I accompanied German DJ Paul Kalkbrenner for a week on his tour. My accreditation said 'band psychologist'. Paul is football mad. I had met him a year before and, for our wedding anniversary, my wife had given me a meet-and-greet ticket to his summer concert, and he had in turn attended a Champions League game. Winning the FA Cup had given us hope for a new, golden era at Arsenal, but the 2014/15 season got off to a rocky start. Mesut and I had come back late from holiday, and the French section of the team, who had also reached the quarter-finals, were just as tired. We only managed to win two of our first eight games and had to write off the championship once more after the first half of the season. Again, the objective became just to finish in the top four. In the end, 75 points got us into third place behind Chelsea and City. We had achieved no more than the bare minimum. On the upside, we made it once more into the final of the FA Cup. Like Hull before them, Aston Villa had only managed to avoid relegation by a narrow margin, so everyone was expecting us to deliver an easy win. Just like the previous year, we were staying at a hotel right next to Wembley. Morning breakfast gave us a direct view of the ground. The atmosphere was strange. Later, from our windows, we could see the masses passing by the building and hear the fan park bass humming in the distance. Boom, boom, boom. No chance of a pre-game nap.

On the pitch, everything went exactly as we'd hoped for a change. We were vastly superior. Christian Benteke didn't get a single chance the entire game. From the very first minute, there was only one team in control. 1-0, Theo Walcott before the break. 2-0, Alexis Sánchez. 4-0, Olivier Giroud. Hang on. Isn't there a goal missing? Indeed. Benteke hadn't managed to keep up with my pace in the box, and I scored the third after a corner.

As captain, I accepted the trophy. During the second half of the season, I had been wearing the armband constantly, if only on behalf of Arteta, who had been out of action due to various small injuries. Unfortunately, it rained hard the next day, which took the shine off the celebrations. While a second cup win was a great success, the fans were still craving a league title. They could have got one in 2015/16, too. Many top teams were having issues. Champions Chelsea were stuck mid table and sent Mourinho packing; Liverpool sacked Brendan Rogers and replaced him with Jürgen Klopp; United were struggling under Louis van Gaal; and City were having difficulties with Manuel Pellegrini, as they waited for Pep Guardiola to arrive the following season.

Surprisingly, Leicester made it to the top of the league, with us following closely behind. There was a feeling that Claudio Ranieri's side was going to collapse at some point. In mid-February, it was time for a showdown at the Emirates. Things went back and forth constantly, it was if the game was played without any midfielders. When Danny Welbeck scored the winning goal in the fifth minute of injury time, the stadium exploded. We were top of the league. Now, we only had ourselves to beat. And that's exactly what we ended up doing. In the next game, away at Manchester United, we let ourselves be caught out by an eighteen-year-old who, until then, no one had heard of. Marcus Rashford scored twice, and we lost 3-2.

I was only on the bench, which explained everything. In all seriousness, though, we might have allowed our senses to be clouded a bit too much by that post-Leicester euphoria. In the Premier League, you start every game from zero and have to bring an unwavering intensity if you want a chance of winning. We should have been prepared for Manchester wanting to rain on our parade, but we weren't. The defeat turned all our energy upside down. We lost 2-1 at home to Swansea and drew 2-2 with Tottenham in our following two games. Suddenly the title was out of reach for us. Leicester ended up winning the league. On the last day of the season, we managed to finish second, making it the twenty-first consecutive time we ended a season ahead of Spurs. While keeping the upper hand in North London was important to the fans, it didn't really bring comfort to anyone after such a missed opportunity. Where had we gone wrong? As a team, we should have simply played better in crucial moments. Simple as that. Every team has its poor phases over the season, the trick is minimising them. You have to draw quick lessons from defeats and immediately remind yourself of your own strengths. Other teams were better at that. They managed setbacks better, not letting themselves be intimidated by those first negative waves, and ignoring what people on the outside were saying. We didn't have the ability to shift quickly and keep our faith after a disappointment. When we lost one game, we often lost a few in a row. We could show off our class across six FA Cup games, but 38 league matches in ten months were a different matter. We simply lacked the consistency all top teams need. You couldn't win the league on eight defeats a year. Arsène Wenger was always the kind of manager whose belief in his team's qualities was steady as a rock and who approached matters with never-ending patience. He didn't lose his nerve during losing streaks, either. He stuck with his convictions and his players, no matter how strong the wind was blowing. It was his greatest strength.

Wondering whether it was also his greatest weakness and whether he was he too lenient with us is, in my opinion, a little too simplistic. If the fans had had their way, there would have been five new top signings every year. 'Spend some fucking money!' they would chorus from the stands after defeats. But Wenger trusted the players he had. I never met another manager who believed more strongly in his squad's ability. In 2015/16, he didn't buy a single outfield player — just a new 'keeper, Petr Čech — because he was convinced that the squad was good enough to win the title. People were beside themselves, but Wenger was thinking on a deeper level:

What happens to my starting forward if I add a new one? Is that really going to improve the team, or would I be unsettling my best man? Is five people fighting for the same position a good thing?

First and foremost, Wenger saw us as human beings, and he had a lot of faith in us, which is why he stood by us. Ultimately, we as players need to ask ourselves whether we did everything possible to justify his trust. Did we implement his instructions perfectly? Were we pulling together? Did we learn from our mistakes? No. Wenger has won three Premier League titles; which is proof enough of his standing as a manager. The team, on the other hand, had fallen short since 2004.

Click, click, click. There it was again, the worst sound in professional sport. After a run-of-the-mill pass during a friendly against RC Lens in July 2016, my right knee began to creak. The pain was minor, but the knee swelled up quickly. Cartilage damage: a break of several months before the season had even begun. After the operation, I had to wear a splint for six weeks, no walking allowed. For the length of those six weeks, I moved back into my parents' house. It was weird being back in my old room at 31, but I tried to make the best of it, watching the Olympics, reading Stephen King's *It*, and having school friends over for a game of cards. Lots of water, little food — my goal was to lose a few kilos before rehab, so that I wouldn't need to exercise away the fat first.

The phone rang. Arsène Wenger. I was braced for bad news, but he informed me that I would be Arsenal captain with immediate effect, even if I wasn't going to be playing for a long time. 'You're an important figure at this club,' he said. 'You're my first choice.'

I hadn't thought that was going to happen. Normally, a manager wants his captain in the team. And you yourself want to be on the pitch, too, helping people, making a difference. But sometimes, you just have to interpret this role differently, and I was convinced I could do it without pretending. It was what Wenger wanted.

'Just be yourself,' he said. 'You don't need to overdo it or force anything.'

After three months in Donaustauf, I returned to London. It took a very long time, nearly nine months, for the muscle mass to regenerate and for me to feel secure about my knee. The fact that Wenger had made me captain in my darkest hour was a great motivation. Under no circumstances did I want to let a whole season pass by during which I, as captain, didn't spend a single minute on the pitch. I kept going through my routine and tried to give everything in training, including calibrating the mood in the dressing room. There are different ways to lead a team. You don't have to thump your chest; it also works with self-mockery and a certain twinkle in your eye. For me, it was important to surprise the boys every now and then. Danny Welbeck, for example, couldn't believe that at 32, I knew Drake tracks off by heart. The dressing room was ringing with laughter. You have to engage with the younger generation, show them you can relate. There's no point in constantly walking around with a wagging finger or just dwelling on what it was like 'in your day'.

These days, you need to connect with the lads on a different level, even if that includes special handshakes. In February, I was summoned by Wenger and then-CEO Ivan Gazidis. The first thing they asked was whether I wanted to stay at the club beyond the end of the season. I did — as a player, that is. But the two of them suggested something else. Could I imagine taking over the Academy once my playing career had ended in the summer of 2018? I went to Oliver Bierhoff for advice. 'Do it,' he said. But first, I needed the boss's blessing. Ulrike's. When we had moved to England, the agreement had been that we would return to Germany at the end of my playing career, to a city of her taste and choosing, so that she may do what she pleased. It was supposed to be a kind of compensation for her giving up her handball career for me. But the feedback was positive: we were happy in London, the kids were happy at school, and we had a circle of friends. She wanted us to stay, too. I began to delve into the subject of academy work, reading numerous books, and comparing notes with experts. The plan was to get my B licence in autumn 2017, but I was desperate to return to the pitch before then. Once again, 2016/17 was one of those seasons during which, unfortunately, the mood was set early on: we were eliminated from the Champions League in the round of sixteen by Bayern and fell badly behind in the title race; we were even in danger of not finishing fourth in the league. For the final phase of the season, Wenger switched to a back three to ensure more coverage without the ball, and while that helped the team, it was less than ideal for me.

During March and April 2017, I had been in the squad a few times, but now, even though I felt fit, I wasn't being considered at all. Two weeks before the end of the season, I realised I wouldn't be playing another game. The race for fourth place had been decided against us and for the first time in Wenger's tenure, we had missed out on the Champions League. And while, surprisingly, we had managed to make it into the FA Cup final again with a win over Manchester City, my participation there was out of the question. Suddenly feeling awfully tired and worn out, I found myself asking existential questions. I went to Wenger to inform him of this and ask whether he might possibly release me for an early holiday.

'Boss, you're not playing me, no matter how well or otherwise I do in training,' I said. 'I'm not given a chance to prove myself, and it's getting me down.'

'I know it's hard,' he replied. 'But you have to remain prepared; your chance could come anytime.' And sure enough, Kieran Gibbs got injured during final training before the last home game against Everton. *Okay,* I thought, *this way, you'll at least be able to watch the last game from the bench.* Koscielny was sent off after fourteen minutes, but we were still leading 2-0 after the first half. No problem at all. Until, that is, Gabriel had to be stretchered off with a severe ligament injury. Wenger glanced over his shoulder, probably wondering whether to bring on assistant manager Steve Bould, who might have been 54 but used to be a very good defender. Wenger must have noticed me from the corner of his eye.

'Now, you'll have to go on,' he said. I had not been prepared for this at all. It had been clear to me from the start that I wouldn't be called into action; there was no tension left in my body. But by now, the score was only 2-1, and Everton had brought on Romelu Lukaku. Would my knee hold up? Matches are entirely different from training, because in addition to the increased physical load, there was a certain pressure, an expectation you placed on yourself. The last thing I wanted was for the team to have to carry me or for me to have to be subbed off after five minutes. That had been Mikel Arteta's fate for a long time: as captain, he had been desperate to return to the pitch, and when the time had come, his hamstring had let him down after five minutes and he'd had to come straight off. It finished him, and I didn't want the same to happen to me. Would I able to make another comeback without risking my health so much that I might not be able to play with my kids anymore? My mind was buzzing, but I managed to block out those thoughts during the game. It had always been one of my strengths. Going from one action to the next, doing the simple things I had always done, trying to win tackles, and playing a simple ball — that approach carried me to the final whistle. In the end, we won the match and I took a forty-minute lap of honour in front of friends, family, and our physios. It was a fantastic ending. We might have finished fifth, but after that horror show of a season, I was glad to have contributed at least once. The feeling I enjoyed most was realising that I was still able to play at a Premier League level and help the team, when ten days previously, all I wanted had been to drive to a beach somewhere and never come back. The knowledge that in football, things could change at the speed of light was far from new, but this episode proved very motivational to me over the coming days.

It was a suspenseful time. The regulars at the back were either injured or suspended, so Wenger didn't have many options left. Still, he had the option of switching to a back four and leaving me out. After all, ninety minutes in the FA Cup final against Chelsea, the best team in the country, was different from forty minutes against an Everton side that had already been in holiday mode. I caught myself preparing to sit on the bench. On the other hand, it was Wembley. I had won games there with Germany in 2007 and 2013, scoring one of my rare international goals in the former. With Arsenal, I had won three out of three FA Cup semi-finals and lifted the trophy twice. So why shouldn't the third final go just as well? Just the thought of that ground with its tall arch made the sun rise inside me. Yes, Chelsea were favourites, but so what? It was Wembley.

At final training, I was given a yellow bib and knew I would be part of the big day, at the centre of a back three with Rob Holding and Nacho Monreal. The last resorts, if you will. Before the Everton match, I had last played that position in Pattensen's youth, as sweeper. Arsenal were depleted and not exactly in great shape. The experts couldn't seem to agree: would Chelsea get a quiet victory, or would they walk all over us? We were the heavy underdog; no one backed us to come out on top. There was concern internally, too, worry that we were going to be steamrollered. Eden Hazard would surely too good for us. The agitation was palpable. In the days and hours before kick-off, though, a kind of now-more-than-ever mentality developed in the dressing room. 'We can do this!' It was clear that everyone had to push their limits; everyone had to work for the others, more so than usual.

The one thing we tried to remember was that on a good day, we were able to beat any team in the world. Both in training and during the video analysis sessions, we prepared well for Chelsea's way of playing. The Blues really made use of their wingers and their routines were well-rehearsed, particularly those between Hazard and Diego Costa, their centre-forward. We were going to focus on disrupting the supply between them. The club psychologist suggested we record video messages for each other before the game. Two years previously, he had players' relatives do exactly that for the team.

Just before a Cup final kicks off, Wembley is usually bustling with activity. The national anthem plays. Sometimes, paratroopers will land on the pitch, on other occasions, the military will fire gun salutes. As captain, you present your team to dignitaries on the red carpet: Prince William shook my hand. I enjoyed myself immensely. There were giant flame throwers positioned on the touchline that gave off so much heat that I was worried about my eyebrows.

We were intent on ignoring all the chatter and using the game's momentum to our advantage. For a good ten minutes, we held on to the ball, allowing our defence to settle and familiarise ourselves with the situation. We managed to keep danger away from our own goal, and our dominance led to a chance or two. Before Chelsea had got into the game properly, Sánchez put us in the lead. Immediately, the fans' fear dissolved. It turned into a magical afternoon. We had a good grip on Diego Costa. The German broadsheet *Süddeutsche Zeitung* once described him as 'a toxic irritant in shorts', and he was indeed a master at infuriating defenders with many little acts of violence and provocation. Rob Holding and I kept him in check with a 'good cop, bad cop' routine: Rob dished it out both verbally and physically, while I put an arm around Costa and shouted encouragements.

Despite our best efforts, he equalised twenty minutes before the end, but it ended up not mattering. Nothing and no one was going to stop us and, no sooner had Chelsea drawn level, Aaron Ramsey was down the other end, putting us ahead again. And that was it: an outstanding game from back to front, which we thoroughly deserved to win. My first appearance in the starting eleven that season ended with me hoisting the cup in the royal box. It was a unique moment, a little football fairytale. Was there anyone left who had still believed I could give that kind of performance? Probably only Arsène Wenger. Ahead of the final, Martin Keown had expressed his doubts about my level of performance, just like many others. After the match, I bumped into him in the tunnel. 'Don't write me off, Martin,' I said. 'Ever.'

'The game will go down in history as the Mertesacker final,' he replied sheepishly.

The trust Wenger and my peers had placed in me was humbling. My teammates were genuinely happy for me, and in turn, all of us were happy for Wenger, who followed up his seventh FA Cup victory with a new two-year contract. Was this, then, not the best moment to exit the stage, at Wembley, bathed in sunlight? Not for me, no. I had assured the club I would play on for another year. And in any case, I had tasted blood: after the win against Chelsea, I was feeling far too good to hang up my boots. In the end, I only played a few times during the 2017/18 season, but I enjoyed the time with the team in the knowledge that soon, memories would be all I had left of it. I no longer saw myself able to play regular games at the highest level.

In September 2017, something highly embarrassing happened. For the first (and last) time, I missed training without permission. After a defeat to Stoke, we were due two days off, but Wenger had scheduled a session on short notice. Everyone was to be back on Monday afternoon. I was in Germany, with a flight booked for Monday morning, something I would never have done under normal circumstances. What's the worst that could happen? And of course, the worst happened. My flight was cancelled because of a technical problem. I had to phone Wenger, feeling incredibly awkward that I, as captain, should miss a training session. The next day, I told him to slap me with a fine. I paid £10,000 into the team fund and had learned another life lesson: never rely on others during urgent engagements. Thinking back to my playing days at Arsenal, they seem to tell an epic story — which is quite true — and it's good that it finished before it could come to a bitter ending. Carrying on wasn't an option; my knee wouldn't have been able to bear it. My body was exhausted, my batteries empty.

I was desperate to avoid a situation where my sons would have to face questions from the many Arsenal fans at school as to why their dad was playing so poorly. Thanks to my new role at the club, my family and I had been given another chance to settle in London. We identify with the city and all that comes with it, both positive and negative. Compared to Bremen and Hannover, the cost of living here is shocking: food costs four times as much, and the rent is absurd. We keep asking ourselves how people do it, families where the father doesn't play professional football. So far, we haven't found an answer.

For a sense of home, we talk to our children in German, even though their English is perfect. We also visit the German Christmas market at Waterloo or maybe an Oktoberfest and celebrate Christmas on 24 December. We do a lot to maintain our German culture, but at the same time, we're glad that at school, the kids meet other children from all around the world, from all kinds of religious backgrounds. Thirty-five percent of the population are foreign. To our kids, that's as normal as it is for all Londoners.

We're anxious to see what happens after Brexit. In the capital, an overwhelming majority voted to remain; we're living in a bubble. In less affluent areas, people believed that without the EU, things would improve. Politicians appealed to the national pride, promising heaven on earth. And blue passports. To me, it was shocking that such sensible, sober people like the British could fall for this propaganda. In reality, many promises would either cost billions of pounds or cannot be kept at all. I believe no one who voted to leave was aware of the astronomical costs that would come with such a step. My father had seen it coming. Before the vote, he advised me to remove my savings from London and exchange them into euros, just to be safe. A day after the referendum, the price of the pound crashed by ten percent.

What will become of us and the kids in the medium term? I truly hope that the Brits will emerge relatively unscathed from this self-imposed misery.

Ulrike and I still catch ourselves yearning for some nice German bread rolls, but over time, we've come to take a more relaxed approach to life in England. It's not like Germany, where things that need sorting are sorted immediately. If there's a lamp askew in the stairway, chances are you have to wait three weeks for the caretaker to set it straight. Without this kind of calm, life in a place like London would probably be impossible, so you end up accepting it. The number of people going about their business never ceases to amaze me, just like the number of people who squeeze themselves into train carriages and still manage to apologise politely if they so much as bump into someone. Elsewhere, these masses might trigger a stampede.

I'm very much looking forward to the new rhythm: less travelling, more time with my family, and more time to discover London and the UK properly. So far, we haven't even managed to visit Plymouth or Cornwall. Or Scotland, for that matter — I am a big *Braveheart* fan. I would love to see all these places in person and learn about the history; maybe go look for the Loch Ness Monster, visit Stonehenge, or take the Eurostar to Disneyland Paris. Thanks to my busy schedule, we didn't manage to do a single one of those things in seven years. Life will slow down, or at least I hope it will. I doubt it's going to do so a lot, though. There is so much to do for Ulrike and me every day that we coordinate our appointments on a board by the front door. There are clear rules for the kids: mandatory family breakfast at

7.30 followed by tooth brushing and getting dressed, then off to pre-school at 8.15. Leave the house any later and you won't get a good parking spot.

4

WELTMEISTER

GERMANY 2006

I JOINED THE NATIONAL TEAM IN OCTOBER 2004.
Back then, I was still living in Pattensen with my parents. The squad was to meet in Munich, and I was slightly surprised that Thomas Brdarić and I were being picked up at the airport by a driver. I had no idea how much more public interest the national team attracted compared to Hannover 96. But we were well protected from all the noise and hubbub: one interview a day, then you were left well alone. The staff were extremely caring, including the physios and masseurs. The atmosphere in general was very good back then; I immediately got the feeling I belonged.

After training, there was always time to retreat, time to reflect on what was going on. As a novice, I had to give a speech in front of the entire team. I can't remember my exact words, but everyone tends to say the same things in moments like that: how they've been made to feel welcome, how they want to thank the manager for putting his trust in them, and so on. In my case, that approach was probably preferable to being forced to sing. The speech was the official part. You knew you were part of something. Now, you belonged to that inner circle, to those few who'd made it. You looked around and there was Oliver Kahn. For me as a youngster, the situation demanded respect. Not to mention the new managers, all new characters whom I was meeting in person for the very first time. It was extraordinary. Nevertheless, I wasn't awestruck. In Brdarić, I had an ex-Hannover colleague by my side, which meant a lot. On your own, you might lose yourself in that collection of stars and egos.

Back then, Thomas Hitzlsperger was new to the team, too, which helped. That way, I wasn't alone during the press conference: there was someone sitting next to me for whom all this was also a first. It made the whole thing easier, spreading the attention around. We trained for a few days before flying to Tehran to play Iran. It was new for me, and I remember how sore I was, because we had been doing stabilisation exercises that targeted muscle groups previously unknown to me. Suddenly, you were jumping around the pitch with these rubber bands strapped to your legs and being subjected to great resistance. Everything hurt, but hey, I was with the national team! I had to prove myself again.

My goal was to stick with it for as long as possible. I tried surviving the training sessions; my first thought being *Please don't let me make a mistake*. I didn't necessarily want to be on the receiving end of all the passes, either. But I still had good reason to stay calm: Klinsmann and Löw's instruction was to keep the ball low at the back. We practiced it again and again. It was convenient for me, because I didn't know any other way. My aim had always been to win the tackle and then play a neat and simple pass. I didn't need to change my game; I had always played the same way, be it at the Academy, with the Under-23s, or in the Bundesliga.

The streets of Tehran were so dusty that you couldn't see more than fifty metres ahead from inside the bus. It was an unfamiliar world. During final training, Iranian women handed us roses. There is a picture of me standing next to a woman with a rose, a look of confusion all over my face. It was simply too much for me, all these things that I had never seen before and certainly hadn't been expecting. A hundred thousand people filled the stadium. There were no seats, no tickets were bought in advance, and the place was packed five hours before kick-off. We had been told that women were going to enter the stadium in disguises, because officially they weren't allowed to watch football in Iran. The atmosphere was surreal. I think both that trip and the friendly were part of a deal to acquire votes for the hosting of 2006 World Cup. Iran played Ali Karimi, who put on quite a show. He worked his magic until the final whistle, and I think Bayern signed him straight after the match. We still won the match, though, thanks to goals from Fabian Ernst and Thomas Brdarič. I played the last ten minutes, because Christian Wörns had suffered an injury. There was no time for me to warm up; things went too quickly for me. The crowd were braying, so much so that I couldn't really enjoy myself. *Please don't let me make a mistake,* I thought. *Please let me get through this.* It was the only thing on my mind. Those ten minutes were crucial, ten minutes without a mistake.

With the final whistle came the joyful realisation that the coach had given me playing time. It showed me that I wasn't just there to survive the training. No, I actually made an appearance, and in front of that kind of crowd. At the post-game banquet I received a medal as souvenir for my first international. Very early in my career, moments like that stayed with me. I had to find out for myself whether or not I would be able to cope with them. In addition, there was the fact that after Tehran, I had to return to the Under-21s for a Euro qualifier. It meant yet another new environment, another new team. Altogether, I played three or four games for the Under-21s. Fortunately, I didn't get stuck there the way some young players do. My performance against Iran had earned me a spot with the seniors, something that certainly wasn't assured at the time. I was only twenty years old. At that age, it usually took a hundred Bundesliga matches to even be considered. It was Jürgen Klinsmann who shelved that way of thinking. He knew that in order to be able to use young players at the 2006 World Cup, he would have to introduce them purposefully two years before and play them regularly. Giving them two games just before the tournament would not have worked. Klinsmann's approach was a stroke of luck for our generation — for Thomas Hitzlsperger, Robert Huth, Bastian Schweinsteiger,

Lukas Podolski, and me.

The general feedback was very positive. The *Hannoversche Presse* ran the headline, 'Our man for Germany'. My parents were very proud of me, but more than anything, they were terribly pleased for me. After everything people had said about me in my youth, after all my physical problems at fifteen, this path could not have been foreseen by anyone. Going from sneers of, 'You won't make it, anyway,' to German international in five years had not been a likely development, not even close. But I didn't get the feeling of having made it. My parents raised me differently. *Football is nice, but it's not everything. We don't have just one son but three.* This perspective always brought me back down to Earth. Apart from that, the most important thing being an international brought with it was the responsibility of living up to expectations. Before, I had somehow slipped into professional football via Hannover's Academy, but now, with the eagle on my chest, I had become a figure of identification, which meant a whole different kind of scrutiny.

The enthusiasm broke out in Germany after the 2005 Confederations Cup, where we finished third. There was a feeling of having the entire country behind us, despite the media's qualms about Klinsmann's attacking style and the concerns about our inexperience. The tournament had been littered with goals, both for and against us, but there was no stopping the euphoria. Sometimes, the media enjoy trying to cast doubts over a team's capabilities, but here, they were unsuccessful.

At least they were until we lost 4-1 to Italy in Florence in March 2006. We were entirely out of sorts during that match.

We had no control whatsoever and no proper strategy; there was no agreement between the different parts of the team. We were being overrun at the halfway line. No one knew what was going on; it was a terrible feeling. We were trailing 3-0 at half-time, and I was substituted. Later, during drug testing, I found myself next to Alessandro Del Piero, who was helping himself to food from the buffet, a portion of ham on his plate. It was ideal, because my Italian skills were limited to exactly one word: *prosciutto*, and so that's what I said to him. That one word. He nodded and continued eating. That was the entire sum of our conversation. In this moment, after such a disappointing match, it was comforting to see that Del Piero, a man from the great, wide world of football, was simply standing around, cramming ham into his mouth. I was amazed by this normality. It felt great and allowed me to forget our catastrophic performance quickly. *It was only one match. Let's look ahead.*

The reactions in Germany, however, were harsh. *Kicker* handed me a 5.5, and in his column, Paul Breitner called for the reintroduction of the sweeper. The consensus was that we wouldn't play a successful World Cup with this defence, not with that Mertesacker kid who was too tall — and more importantly, too slow — and especially with Klinsmann in charge. For the first time, we appreciated just how high the stakes were. The fact that Klinsmann had nearly been sacked due to pressure from the tabloids, though, was something we only realised after the tournament had ended. At the time, we didn't know how precarious his situation really was. Jürgen remained positive throughout, even after the bitter defeat to Italy. It had been made even plainer to us how hard we had to work until the World Cup in order to achieve stability in our game. The discussion about the defence had been around already. Was it good enough? Were the right players in the right positions? There was a constant stream of questions, and they were all validated by that performance in Florence. That couldn't happen again and so, to avoid the negativity, we tried to use the defeat in a useful way. 'Okay, that was an away game, but the World Cup's going to be in Germany.' Jürgen had always stressed the fact that the tournament was our final destination and that the road leading up to it would be bumpy, full of both good and bad experiences. We were an inexperienced side, but he said he would harden us up in time for the start of the World Cup, and we believed him.

It was especially important to Klinsmann to make young players part of the trip, and to him, that meant involving their parents. Before a friendly against South Africa in September 2005, he had invited my parents to Bremen for a chat. Initially, I didn't see the point. I was already a professional, so where did my parents fit in? He wanted to get to know the family and assure them that he was looking after the young players in his squad. At the same time, he wanted to assess their domestic situation. But more than anything, he wanted to make very clear that this would be *the* year. For him, it was important that the parents knew that their son might play at a World Cup and to brace themselves for a turbulent time. The fact that the national team manger made time for a player's parents when he was already an adult left a mark on me. I had never seen it done before, and it impressed me. My parents were touched, too. It was one of the most remarkable actions by a coach beyond the pitch I have ever witnessed.

In the run-up to the World Cup, the defensive positions were still up for grabs and, for a long time, it wasn't clear who would be playing. Initially, Christian Wörns was still under consideration, and Jens Nowotny eventually joined the squad as fourth defender, but the shortlist consisted of Robert Huth, Christoph Metzelder, and myself. Of course, we were watching each other closely — how does this player approach this situation, how does that player move across the pitch? The final decision was made just before the first group match: Metzelder and I would be starting at the tournament. It was a good moment, but it was also time to pay back the trust put in me, to actually implement everything we had built over the last two years. Klinsmann was the head of the operation, the motivator. He approached everything with immense enthusiasm, providing the momentum.

But it was Jogi who was the tactical genius, taking a backseat and working explicitly with the defence. His level of knowledge was noticeable immediately; it earned him a lot of trust among the team. He knew how to arrange a defence properly and how to position players. All of that was Löw. While he didn't talk much in the beginning, not even in team meetings, that changed over the following years. In small groups, though, he was always good, and his speeches were always articulate. Our basic principle was backing each other up. We won't allow balls behind the defence, we won't be outplayed. If we see someone able to play a clear ball, we'll retreat. And if the other team is in possession out on the left, we'll always position ourselves in a way that will protect our teammate's back. As a player, that strategy helped me evolve. I learned not just to look at a single opponent but at the opposition as a whole.

Metzelder was my first contact on the pitch, my partner in crime. We were in this together. Behind us, Jens Lehmann commanded the defence. He was very demanding. He gave very clear orders to push up or stay deep. But we had a good feeling about him, because he was active, never shy to come off his line. Back then, he was already more of a sweeper 'keeper, which made him the great exception within his generation. For almost two years, the coaching staff speculated about the best goalkeeper for our game. It was common knowledge that Oliver Kahn was outstanding on the line and powerful when he came out for the ball. He swept everything out of his way. But there was still a hunch that a decision would be made in favour of Jens. Eventually, Kahn lost his captain's armband and the DFB hired a new goalkeeping coach in Andreas Köpke. Sepp Maier, Kahn's companion from Munich, was gone: he had been too close to Bayern for Klinsmann's taste. Despite this setback, Oliver was crucial to the team's structure. He had confronted the competition, always ready to give his all.

He faced everything with a smile, too, probably because he already had an idea how things would pan out. Nonetheless, he never let himself go and continued to go full throttle. If, say, Lehmann managed 55 push-ups during a performance test, Kahn did everything he could to beat that score. With his last ounce of strength, he would conjure up push-up number 56. He was very well respected, in part because he would stay behind at the dinner table to share his stories with us younger players. He gave us insights into his career, including his private life — his marriage, his girlfriend, etc. To me as a youngster, it was fascinating. You would sit there listening, not saying a word.

Ultimately, Klinsmann and Löw opted for the more modern 'keeper. In hindsight, you could say that the signs had been pointing in that direction for two years: the coaching staff simply wanted to try something different. Fortunately, the rivalry between Jens and Oliver didn't have an adverse effect on the squad. The two of them simply kept out of each other's way and didn't talk much during training, either. I don't think they even warmed each other up before games; Andreas Köpke put in extra shifts instead. There weren't any problems in the squad in general, no great tensions. A manager will always want the highest level of rivalry, of course, but it does help if there are people on the team who understand and accept their roles. That applied to players like Thomas Hitzlsperger, Mike Hanke, Oliver Neuville, Sebastian Kehl, and Marcell Jansen, who were on standby, ready to give everything in training and for their country. They did their bit. Back then, the coaching staff team was smaller, and their jobs were very well defined.

I benefited immensely from Jürgen Klinsmann, because he was so supportive of the next generation. 'We need new players, a breath of fresh air,' he said. Oliver Bierhoff was good to me, too. He saw something in me from the beginning. Personality development was one of his major issues. He approached me and said, 'You've got your *Abitur*, you're interested in things; I'll send some books your way. Give them a read.' At times, it would be an abstract topic like leadership; at others, a novel like Thomas Mann's *Buddenbrooks*. One or two of them helped me work on myself and put things in a wider and greater context. Bierhoff kept goading me, nudging again and again. He wanted to give me more than football would be able to; he didn't want my horizon to end at the touchline. As director, Bierhoff always kept an eye on the bigger picture. He made an effort to get across the true meaning of major tournaments. 'With mind and heart,' was his mantra before each game. We were supposed to play purposefully and deliberately while at the same time being fiery and passionate. In the meantime, the pressure rose quickly.

The World Cup in our country was drawing closer and closer, and we knew we had to make a good impression. We knew we had eighty million people to convince. Those thoughts festered away in our minds, and the DFB were trying all they could to make sure we would be able to cope. The concrete preparations were very detailed on a level that, presumably, no one had considered before. Chief DFB scout Urs Siegenthaler had prepared a dossier for the opening game: what are the customs in Costa Rica, how do the people live, what do they eat, when do they go to sleep? We were supposed to understand the way culture and local events were expressed through their game. 'They see losing possession as an attack on their honour,' Siegenthaler explained. 'They'll want to win it back as quickly as possible.' I can't say how exactly this information helped us on the pitch, but learning about these correlations, thinking about them just a bit, was definitely new and interesting to me. The concept worked, so it was repeated again and again. To this day, a slightly diluted version of those little ethnology seminars is still in practice.

From my work with Ralf Rangnick, I was already familiar with video analysis but not to the extent to which it was used by the national team, where the material was very clear. Over time, the subject became even more specialised. Before the group matches, TV journalist Marcel Reif was invited to explain what we were to expect from the media. Strictly speaking, it was not media training but rather an advisory event. Who and what is dangerous? What is safe? What could you do, what shouldn't you do? '*Kicker* is quite harmless, but watch out for the tabloids,' Reif said. 'Don't read too much of that stuff, and don't let it influence you.' It was very important to the coaching staff that we be well prepared for possible media traps and stories that tend to be created during such tournaments. As a young player, I had never been told anything like that. After my first games for Hannover, I had simply stood in front of a crowd of journalists and told them whatever was on my mind.

It was clear that we were going to be unable to disengage ourselves completely from the coverage. There is always a lot of interest in the papers' player ratings; it has always been like this, and it probably won't change. But we were advised to try and forget these things as quickly as possible, everything that came in from the outside and wasn't beneficial to our work. The good thing for players like me was the fact that Schweini and Poldi attracted the most interest, as did Michael Ballack's troublesome calf prior to the Costa Rica game: *Wade der Nation,* they called it — the calf of the nation. In the run-up to the World Cup, Ballack had made the conscious decision to engage with the press as little as possible, because he wanted to focus entirely on the games and his role as leader. He was an absolute alpha. When Michael Ballack told us to turn left, we all turned left. He was tough. He was the *capitano*, and everybody knew it. At the same time, though, Ballack didn't shy away from handing out praise and getting everyone on board. His lieutenant was Torsten Frings, as Kahn's demotion had altered the team's hierarchy.

I found myself under less scrutiny thanks to the hype around Schweini and Poldi, the *duo infernale*, who were the stars of Sönke Wortmann's *Deutschland. Ein Sommermärchen,* a film that documented Germany's World Cup campaign in its entirety. The two of them were inseparable and coped well with the hubbub. They were comfortable in the spotlight, and the rest of the group didn't have an issue with that — on the contrary. *Let them be*, we thought to ourselves. *That way, we're left in peace and get to focus on our concerns.* It played into my hands; I was able to prepare undisturbed and spend a lot of time, for example, on treating my heel troubles. Jens Nowotny introduced me to *World of Warcraft*, which was a good way to escape reality. Nowadays, hotels with wifi are standard, but back then it was all a novelty. I would sit in my room with a laptop, assuming the identity of an elf archeress. An assassin. Petite, quick, and slinky — all the things, in short, that I am not.

In general, I was fine with the pressure. Of course, on matchdays, I went to the toilet more often than usual; the difference to regular working days was immense. But I kept interpreting it the same way. *This is fine. It has to be this way so you're focused. Yes, you're incredibly agitated, but use that tension to build up your concentration.* One thing that usually helped me was singing the national anthem. Loudly. It reduced my nervousness. In that moment, you realise once again what is at stake, but I always had a good feeling about the team. When the national anthem was played, I could sense that we were able to count on each other and that we'd be able to deliver a good performance.

Before kick-off against Costa Rica in Munich, we were sitting in the Allianz Arena's dressing room, watching the opening ceremony on TV. It seemed to go on forever. It was the first time I fully appreciated the scale of the event. The longer the show flickered on the screen, the more tense I became. Our eventual 4-2 win didn't remove all doubts. It made us realise our capabilities as a team, but the two goals against us gave a few of the papers the chance to criticise the defence and question my personal suitability. True, we hadn't played well at the back. There had been communication problems between Christoph, Jens, and myself, but I thought the headline *'Schlappwehr'* — limp defence — was unfair. Still, you mustn't let your self-belief be destroyed by the press. After the 1-0 against Poland in our second game in Dortmund, I finally lost my temper over this tone in coverage. Oliver Neuville had scored the last-minute goal, shaking the entire ground, an explosion of joy. During the lap of honour, I looked up into the faces in the press box, only to see nothing but vacant expressions. It was quiet and emotionless. They all just had stupid looks on their faces, something along the lines of, 'Bugger, now we can't write anything negative anymore.' At least, that's how I perceived it in that moment. I made a gesture to say, 'Up yours!'

Never in my life had I been so emotionally charged. In this bubbling cauldron, for the first time ever, I succumbed to a defiant reaction. In that moment, I didn't care one bit whether or not it was appropriate. We had proven we could do better, proven we could keep a clean sheet. We had shown them all. This victory and our qualification for the knockout rounds with a game to spare released a burst of energy. The mood in both the squad and the population was amazing. The atmosphere, the weather, everything was aligned. There were huge fan parks and flags everywhere, it was an entirely new German feeling. The fear that we, team and country, might embarrass ourselves had evaporated, and in place of that anxiety had grown pride and joy. It might sound like a cliché, but this wave of euphoria really carried us; it gave us an incredibly amount of strength.

The DFB made sure we recovered properly between games. Grunewald hotel had a traditional decor, but the association had modern, casual, white furniture moved in to make us feel comfortable. In addition, we were offered table tennis, PlayStation games, and good food. There was a hockey club in the neighbourhood as well as a number of tennis courts, all of which were reserved for us. Occasionally, we went bowling in the evening; the alley was roped off and private. Michael Ballack had organised everything. Apart from that, it was hard to escape the tension. In the hotel, you would automatically think of football, and of preparing for the next game. Unfortunately, we weren't allowed to go anywhere else, not even for dinner at the restaurant. The only opportunity to get out was by driving a few miles at night: Mercedes-Benz had provided us with a fleet of vehicles.

One evening, Tim Borowski and I simply got into one of the cars and sped into the night. No security in tow, nor a camera team. No one saw us; the car was too fast. We rolled down the windows and revved the engine. It gave us a sense of freedom: powering down, then rebooting.

Hochfahren was a word Jürgen Klinsmann used a lot, which related to the need for us to replenish our energy levels between games so we could refocus before our next test.

We won the third match comfortably, beating Ecuador 3-0. Our round of sixteen tie against Sweden took place in Munich, and we played some sublime attacking football. It was madness. We were just as good defensively: Zlatan Ibrahimović made no impression on the game. Our self-belief grew more and more. Back to Berlin. Back to base camp, back to the oasis. More press conferences, more *World of Warcraft*. We had got used to the process. It felt as if the team was getting stronger. Our game against Argentina, though, wasn't a good one. We went 1-0 behind just after half-time and knew our World Cup could be over any second. Argentina played cunningly and clinically; their goal came from a set piece and they defended their lead extremely well. Eventually, Klinsmann brought on Tim Borowski. Michael Ballack shifted to the left to accommodate him and it was from that position where he put in the cross which changed the game. Borowski flicked the ball on at the near post and Miro Klose drifted beyond his marker to equalise. It felt predestined. Our tournament and the country's high couldn't end that day.

But first, of course, there came the shootout. We had practiced penalties intensely in training, with the designated takers hav-

ing to announce where they were going to place their attempt.
I don't think I took part in that particular exercise. 'We'll be the
last ones,' Christoph Metzelder and I had announced. Numbers
ten and eleven, even after Jens Lehmann. Fortunately, neither
of us were needed in Berlin. Our takers were incredibly reliable:
all German penalties were converted. When Esteban Cambias-
so missed, everyone ran towards Jens Lehmann. Everyone apart
from me. I stayed behind in the centre circle, alone with my
thoughts. I couldn't believe what was happening and wanted to
process it. It took a while for me to realise that there were people
celebrating and that I should probably join them.

In that same moment, Argentina's substitutes came onto the
pitch to comfort their colleagues. Suddenly, one of them stood
before me: Leandro Cufré. He kicked me straight in the pri-
vates. The pain made my legs buckle, and around me, an enormous brawl broke out. I'm sure Cufré had mistaken me for Tim
Borowski. Borowski is a great bloke, but he liked to push limits
on the pitch, always wanting to win and always provoking. He
had needled the Argentinians from the minute he had come on
as a substitute, and I suppose had invited their retribution. Tall
and blonde. In Cufré's eyes, the two of us must have looked the
same. Afterwards, the referee came into our dressing room and
asked to see inside my pants. There were six bruises in my gen-
ital area. Cufré was suspended for four games. Laughable. The
subject came up once more three years later, when dear Leandro
signed with Hertha BSC. During his presentation, he apologised
for his actions — presumably under pressure from the club —
but only to the media, not to me. It was of no use to me, and

frankly, I didn't see the point in getting involved. The physical pain from the kick had subsided quickly; what had hurt more and for longer what the fact that Torsten Frings was handed a one-match suspension after a slapping someone in the ensuing melee. Prior to that, though, we celebrated uproariously in the Olympiastadion. Frings did his famous mime, skittling us like bowling pins. It was one of those small details that stayed with me. *Oh, yeah,* I thought. *We could become world champions. We're a tight-knit group.*

Even Oliver Kahn and Jens Lehmann pulled themselves together. When the video screen showed them shaking hands after Lehmann had saved two penalties, the crowd went absolutely wild: we had made it to the semis. The Westfalenstadion again, then. It ended up being another inferno, just like against Poland. The opponent was Italy, and unfortunately, things didn't work out that night. I don't think we played badly; we did have one chance, after all, we just couldn't convert it. The Italians were just a bit more cunning. They defended extremely well, led by Fabio Cannavaro, who would become FIFA World Player of the Year at the end of 2006. Never before had we seen an opposing team display that kind of self-assurance and stability.

Bernd Schneider could have scored. He found himself unmarked in front of goal but could only put the ball over the bar. Finally, they saw us off in extra time; 1-0 after a corner, 2-0 after a counter-attack. My direct opponent was Luca Toni, but I don't remember that much from the game. It's all a blur, really. All I know is that I crumpled after the final whistle. That desperate silence echoing around the ground, it was an eerie moment.

Everyone was shocked. We hadn't prepared for being knocked out of our own World Cup. Sometimes, I wonder what would have happened if the Argentinians had not mistaken me for Tim Borowski: with Torsten Frings, we might have won against Italy and even won the trophy. Oliver Kahn came onto the pitch and whispered in my ear. 'It's not your fault, lad. You've played an outstanding tournament. Be proud of yourself.' And I was. But in that moment, I was also incredibly relieved – relieved that our elimination had not been my fault. The well-being of the entire country no longer depended on me, and, finally, the pain was over. Back at the hotel, though, I was swallowed by emptiness. I fell into nothingness. Everyone felt the same way. We were finished, both physically and mentally; no one was able to sleep. The next day, we needed to rouse our spirits once more: there was still the match for third place. Time to reboot.

A few of us went to the hockey club for some exercise, where we decided to assemble a team and challenge a group of teenagers who were having a match there at the time. We weren't exactly born hockey players, and none of us had any technique — never mind the fact that hockey isn't necessarily the ideal sport for me — but we still went through with it. And while, of course, the kids were superior, we managed to win with a combination of tactical understanding, running quality, and lots of verbal coaching. It was brilliant. We had an incredible day, followed immediately by my decision to have surgery on my ankle. I had suffered with achilles heel pain throughout the entire tournament. Klaus Eder, the national team physio, had helped me through the games. I played on painkillers, which meant I wasn't at a hundred percent. It wasn't like I was in a haze, but my perception was slightly dulled. After surgery, when I returned to the team hotel in Stuttgart a day before the third place play-off, the town centre was full of people. Their excitement and gratitude was overwhelming. We felt like heroes despite the defeat to Italy.

The Portugal game was the perfect happy ending. As reward for their exemplary attitude, Oliver Kahn, Jens Nowotny, Marcell Jansen, Mike Hanke, and Thomas Hitzlsperger were made part of the starting XI. Bastian Schweinsteiger scored two of our three goals. I joined the lap of honour with cast and crutches. It was a wonderful conclusion: even though we hadn't won the Cup, we had still touched many hearts and made Germany proud of its football team again. Suddenly, loving your country was okay again, without aggressions or marginalisation. We had been good hosts and had presented ourselves the way we are.

AUSTRIA & SWITZERLAND 2008

INTERNALLY, WE SUSPECTED JÜRGEN KLINSMANN would leave after the World Cup. He had wanted to introduce new methods, a new culture to spark a fire, and he had managed to do just that. He had paved the way for a new era despite all the sceptics and pencil pushers in the association and opposition from parts of the media. Klinsmann had sacrificed everything; all the while being bombarded with criticism. The tournament had confirmed many of his ideas, but by the end, he was clearly exhausted. Against this backdrop, a change on the bench was the only logical next step. It's somewhat unusual for a manager to come out of nowhere and take over the national team within two years, but Jogi Löw had earned the squad's trust.

I had been very close to him from the start, because he had paid special attention to the defence back in 2006. Meanwhile, I had been playing in Bremen for two years, in a system very much focused on the attack. It was the complete opposite to what I knew from Hannover, where we had sat behind the ball, defended, and waited for counter-attacks. At Bremen, the midfield was generally set up in a diamond, a system that offers much less protection at the back. At times, we would win games 5-4, and on occasions you'd find yourself isolated as a defender. These different styles of play had shaped me, but it was still tremendously helpful to be given some tactical fine-tuning during my time with the national team. It was the squad's wish; we wanted to learn something new. In his playing days, Löw had been a forward and so was able to apply himself in the training of the attack. His broad tactical knowledge meant he was covering all facets. The thought that Jogi himself had not been a great player and so might not have had what it took to manage the national team never occurred to us.

I think as far as Michael Ballack was concerned, it didn't matter who was coaching the team. He was the undisputed captain. Untouchable. No one challenged him. His role and importance to the squad had not changed after the World Cup: he was still the most decisive player and scored the important goals, like the one against Austria during the final group game at the Euros in Austria and Switzerland. Following the 2-1 loss to Croatia during our second game of the tournament, the system had been shifted from the familiar 4-4-2 to a 4-2-3-1, with an additional man in front on the defence in order to increase stability. There were some points of friction within the squad, but the main subject wasn't tactics. It was the way we interacted with each other. Many players no longer felt comfortable with the underlying structure of the team, and that was exacerbated by defeat to Croatia. They were open to criticism but not if it came in a condescending manner or commanding tone.

Things never run completely smoothly over the course of a tournament. Among 23 players, there are always some who feel they're not being appreciated enough. By now, everyone was a star, each with their own entourage and their own opinions. Some wanted more contact with their families between games, other wanted less. Channelling all of that wasn't easy, but back then, we had super characters like Robert Enke and Clemens Fritz, who shaped me a lot. And even though there were more internal controversies compared to the 2006 World Cup, we had a nice time overall. *Bild* came up with the nickname 'Brothers Snore and Creep' for Christoph Metzelder and me. It was not meant to be complimentary. As a player, you can't ignore such things entirely, because they are read by a lot of people.

It's quite annoying and hurts your pride. Naturally, you want to disprove the claims, but with a teammate like Metze, who takes everything in good humour, you cope more easily. We played a lot of basketball in our spare time, so in reaction to *that* headline, we asked Manni Drexler to fix us up with Pau and Marc Gasol's jerseys, two Spanish brothers playing in the NBA. I was Pau, Metze was Marc. Brothers, see? Sure, neither of us were perfect, far from it, but we supported each other and gave it our all. Our bond helped the squad, too. Our team spirit and cooperation on the pitch quelled the effect of the media coverage on the outside.

Following defeat in the final against Spain in Vienna, there was trouble between Oliver Bierhoff and Michael Ballack. Bierhoff wanted the team to hold up a placard reading, *'Danke'*, but Ballack didn't want to participate. It resulted in a heated exchange. A negative outcome after a big game is bound to uncork emotions, maybe even drag up events from the past. And sometimes, alphas just end up locking horns.

We barely had a chance throughout the 90 minutes against Spain. 1-0 sounds marginal, but they were so confident and dominant, and their timing was so perfect, that we couldn't show our potential at all. We were ordered to play with a tight defence, to win the ball, and then to play vertically and quickly on the counter-attack. Our tactics were never that relevant in the final; they weren't what decided the game. Individually, Spain were tremendously strong, and as a team, they were just too talented. Even during set pieces, when we thought we were stronger physically, we never felt dominant. We made small mistakes, there were a few positioning difficulties at the back, and Fernando Torres scored the first goal relatively early. For me, Torres was the best forward around at the time. His movement and the way he held the ball were similar to Robert Lewandowski today. He was insanely fast, too, a complete forward. The lead he gave them made Spain even more confident with the ball and it left us completely powerless. I can't remember us taking a shot at their goal. It would have taken a perfect day to achieve something against this team, and that wasn't the day we were having at all.

Frankly, I was quite glad that the tournament had come to an end. It had been a long few weeks full of tension and pressure. We had spent a lot of time together and had worked really hard. After the final at the Ernst Happel stadium, I stood in the mixed zone, beer in hand, and didn't quite understand why the journalists' perceptions were so negative. I didn't want to have to justify 'only' coming second. We were also criticised for once again making the journey to the fan park in Berlin. How dare we want to be celebrated when we hadn't brought home any silverware?

I thought it was great. The point wasn't to celebrate; we wanted to thank the fans for their support. The national team's popularity had increased dramatically over the years, and we had benefited from that in so many ways. We thought it only right to show our faces in the capital at the end of a tournament, to say a proper goodbye, and to give back to the people.

SOUTH AFRICA 2010

BEFORE THE TOURNAMENT, WE DECIDED ON
this occasion only to go to Berlin if we won the Cup. In the end,
we came third, didn't go to Berlin, and were again met with criticism. We should have shown ourselves one more time, they said.
It was a shame for the fans, they said. We couldn't win.

During qualification, a dream came true: I was back on the
pitch alongside Robert Enke. Playing together for Germany had
always been our wish after I had left Hannover for Bremen in
2006. We had often thought back to it, and when he was recalled
to the national team squad at the age of 29, we would sit in our
room together, before and after games, talking about everything
under the sun. We trusted each other, both on and off that pitch.
We were friends. In April 2009, we beat Wales 2-0 in an important qualifier. Keeping a clean sheet for Germany was one of the
best experiences I had with Robert.

Elsewhere on the pitch during the same game, though, there
was trouble: Lukas Podolski slapped Michael Ballack across the
face. He had disapproved of a command, or rather the tone of it.
I was close by when it happened and broke up the fight immediately. After all, according to the rules it doesn't matter whether
one is struck by an opponent or a teammate, it's still violent conduct. I was afraid there might be one or even two red cards, making things difficult for us. In the heat of the moment, neither of
the two knew what was happening on the pitch. The incident
wasn't good for German football. I tried to make them see sense,

to remind them what was at stake. It was my duty. I don't like it when teammates clash, and I like it even less when things get violent. That attitude of 'You can't tell me what to do' is no help to anyone. Solidarity and success within the team have to come before all else. Exchanging opinions is fine, even if sometimes it's with force, but not like that.

Seven months later, we were sitting at dinner in a Düsseldorf hotel, when Podolski picked up his phone. That moment is seared into my memory; I can see it as if were yesterday. He picked up his phone and showed us a headline. *Robert Enke commits suicide.* Two seconds later, Oliver Bierhoff stood before us and said Robert had thrown himself in front of a train. I heard the words, but they didn't register. They did not make sense. For twenty minutes, no one said a single word. No one touched their food. There were roughly thirty of us sitting there in eerie silence, numb with shock. Then, in the days and weeks that followed, the questions began. How was it possible that this even-tempered, reflective friend was so ill that he took his own life? How was it possible that I hadn't noticed what was going on? And, of course, why had he never told me of his depression? We were friends, were we not, who told each other everything. I thought I knew him. I knew what did him good, but it was not until afterwards that I understood why I had done him good: I had given him a sense of security, and in turn, that feeling had given me immense self-confidence. Whenever I think back, the pain is masked by the joy of those days spent together; by how incredibly impressed I was that he had known me when I joined Hannover's first team in the summer of 2004; by how he was able to place me immediately, even though I had played a mere twenty games; and by the fact that from then on, he let me know that he needed me, that he wanted me to be his teammate. During my first full season in the side, the 2004/05 campaign, Hannover conceded just 36 league goals in 34 games – only two teams conceded fewer. To him, that was the most amazing thing.

The news gave an entirely different, higher meaning to all that. *This person is not coming back. What does that mean? How does it make sense?* Those thoughts spun around in my mind, bothering me. Robert's presence and its effect on me, my career, and my life had been so positive, I could not fathom that he had been fighting a battle with such darkness. I thought I had been close to him. Later, I learned that this kind of concealment is one of the symptoms. Many people suffering from acute depression want to hide it. Most of the time, Robert was the way he had been when I met him: rational, healthy, quietly joyful. Like most of those affected, his depression only caught up with him occasionally and in phases. I think it is important to record this, not to glorify Robert but to clarify that people impacted by depression are in no way weak. It can affect even the strongest, because depression is an illness. The funeral service at Hannover's ground was indescribably sad. Dr Theo Zwanziger – at the time the president of the DFB – gave a very moving speech, during which there came repeated applause from the twenty thousand people in attendance. It was a fitting farewell with many, many tears. I had been to my grandparents' funerals, but losing a friend so soon was a completely new, unfamiliar experience. I cried a lot. In a moment like this, it's probably good not to suppress grief but to let it all out, in order to accept it and to close the chapter. With his death, Robert left us a mission: fight harder against mental illness. Today, many people from his circle campaign on the issue with great dedication, with his wife Teresa at the forefront. I've always been impressed by the way she took on that challenge.

Sometimes, I think it is terrible how quickly everyday life returned to normal. One international fixture was cancelled, but a mere four weeks later, we were back on the pitch, this time in Moscow. Before kick-off, Michael Ballack called on us to look firmly into the Russians' eyes when we walked through the tunnel. Our body language was supposed make it clear to them from the beginning that they wouldn't have any joy against us. 'We'll intimidate them,' he said. 'They can't cope with that.' René Adler played in goal instead of Robert and delivered an outstanding performance.

As a footballer, you always want to look strong. There are few people in this industry who talk a lot about their emotional state or their weaknesses. I was no different. My parents told me I had always sorted things out by myself, no matter the subject, be it school or my girlfriend. Today, we know that not talking can lead to problems. Robert's illness has opened many eyes, encouraging people to engage honestly with their issues and demand help. But it has also held a mirror up to the world of football, showing everyone how little attention is actually paid to mental health. There are so many examples of players who have simply been abandoned. There is so much money at stake in this business that weaknesses, or injuries, are rarely tolerated. Whoever can't contribute to winning the next match is tossed to the side. I am not so naive as to believe things could be inherently different in a world of competition and capitalism. Nevertheless, there needs to be intensive engagement with the down side, and everything needs to be done to ensure that people do not come to harm in that environment. Robert's death was the lowest point of my career. For a short time, I even toyed with the idea of retiring at 28. I discussed it with my peers, too. But there was light at the end of the tunnel, thank God. The prospect of new, exciting challenges kept me in line, and one of those was the chance to play in my second World Cup.

Before the tournament in South Africa, our midfield axis had collapsed. Torsten Frings was no longer under consideration. Michael Ballack had been injured during the FA Cup final, after Kevin-Prince Boateng had tackled him aggressively. René Adler, who was the first choice goalkeeper back then, picked up a rib injury. All three players would not make our final squad, and so an entirely new order had to be formed, with new players such as Sami Khedira, Jérôme Boateng and Holger Badstuber. The attitude within the squad was to wait and see what might happen in South Africa. Those low expectations suited us.

The 4-0 win over Australia in our first match allowed us to find our feet, but that was followed by a 1-0 defeat to Serbia with only ten men for over half the match. Miroslav Klose was sent off, which resulted in a radical change in the group's dynamic. Now we had to win against Ghana. It turned out to be a difficult, hard-fought match, which Ghana could have won if Manuel Neuer had not had one of his best days. In the end we dealt well with the immense pressure well and managed to come out on top in crucial situations. It was Mesut Özil who scored.

During the round of sixteen tie against England in Bloemfontein, the stadium was full of English people. There were England flags everywhere, in that place in the middle of nowhere. It continues to amaze me how many English people follow their team, no matter where they are playing. The ground was firmly in their hands, and David Beckham – who had come to South Africa as an ambassador for England's failed 2018 World Cup bid rather than as a player – joined us in the tunnel. The match went back and forth, but ultimately, we were better. Özil ripped open the left-hand side of the pitch; Thomas Müller always stood in the right spot. It was German quality. Well, quality *and* a little bit of good fortune, seeing as a Frank Lampard's effort hit the bar and clearly landed over the line. It would have been the equaliser and just before half-time. I didn't realise that the goal should have stood during the game, because my view had been obstructed by Manuel Neuer.

Straightaway, I looked at the linesman. *Continue play.* The ball hadn't crossed the line. The scale of the controversy — from England's standpoint, anyway — only hit me after our 4-1 win. The English felt cheated. But in all honesty, that doesn't matter in moments like that. Would it have been possible for Manuel to approach the referee and tell him the ball had gone in? Things went too quickly for that to happen. In any case, Manuel is a clever bloke. Even if the ball had hit the back of the net only to bounce out again, he probably would have tried to play on. He was thinking so fast that he managed to make the linesman think there was no way the ball could have crossed the line. We didn't dwell on it afterwards: mentally, we were already at the next match. *Let's enjoy this time, this feeling.* It was an emotional roller coaster, ridden by a relatively young team.

The same was true of the quarter-finals against Argentina in Cape Town. In the tunnel, prior to kick-off, the Argentinians made a lot of noise. When the teams were lining up, they tried to intimidate us by banging on the walls and screaming in Spanish. At the time, they were favourites for the title. Arne Friedrich, who always stood at the front of the tunnel, turned around and said, 'Men, there's something headed our way.' It stayed with me, just like Diego Maradona and his two watches, dangling from his wrists like saucers. One on the right, one on the left. In the run-up to the match, he had made disparaging remarks about Löw, something along the lines of him not knowing a thing about football. In retaliation, Jogi coached us to destroy El Diego.

He explained to us how Argentina were a divided team: good at the front but less so at the back, and with a gaping hole in midfield. And he was right. Apart from a few problems in the beginning, we defended terrifically, and our counter-attacks were sensational. Even Friedrich scored – our third that day was his first and only goal for Germany and encapsulated the tournament for him. As centre-half, he played a fantastic World Cup. We defended everything, with all available body parts: I took a ball to the face. Argentina could try whatever they wanted, but we wouldn't allow them anything. Lionel Messi in particular despaired, because we had a plan in place against him. I can still hear the words Jogi Löw said during the pre-match meeting: 'Always escort, escort, escort. Don't give him free rein, whatever you do. Don't go down, don't use sliding tackles.' At times, we would block his path with four men; it was a magnificent team performance.

After the 4-0 win against Argentina, the hotel staff in Centurion welcomed us with torches and applause. There was a big party; we simply had to celebrate after a game like that. Special moments like this strengthened our team spirit. There wasn't much to do in our gated community, and there were only a couple of restaurants that we were allowed to visit due to security reasons. Other than that, we barely left the hotel, in part to due the security situation. My daily routine included physiotherapy, watching films with Tim Wiese, and playing table tennis with Piotr Trochowski. On days off, some went sightseeing or on safari, but I couldn't go with them. It would have felt too much as if I was on holiday, and there would be enough time for these things after my career. Michael Ballack had joined up with the squad before the quarter-finals in Cape Town. Shortly afterwards, he told me he would be departing again. 'I don't want to leave you,' he said, 'but I get the feeling I'm out of place here. I can't play, and my presence might be doing more harm than good. I don't want to compromise anyone's performance.' Ballack no longer felt a part of this new team that had evolved over the course of the tournament. The squad had developed a new hierarchy, and he could sense it.

In my opinion, being sensitive enough to recognise this and then withdraw as a result was of great testament to his character. Moments later, Phillipp Lahm declared he wanted to keep the captain's armband beyond the tournament. I found the timing and manner of his statement somewhat strange. For me, Ballack was untouchable at that point. We, and I in particular, owed him so much. As a young player, you're reliant on the old hands, on their trust and their performance. I knew that if the team lost, I in turn would lose my place in it before long. Ballack had always been a dependable force, in all qualifying rounds and tournaments. He was one of those players who shaped the squad to a great extent and who assumed responsibility for success. He deserved our unwavering loyalty, even if he was injured at the time. Hence, I had my reservations about Philipp's initiative. Löw downplayed the matter shrewdly. 'Everyone has ambitions,' he said.

There were discussions within the squad, but it was clear that a decision about the captaincy would only be made after the World Cup. That prevented any issue from festering: Ballack departed, there were no confrontations, and life went on. We were very focused, to the point where the media came up with the thesis that we were only playing as well because Ballack was absent. Of course, new processes come to light when a key player becomes unavailable, and new people get their chance to prove themselves, but football is a team sport. Nothing hinges on a single player. Four days after the game against Argentina, many of those who attributed our strong performance to Ballack's absence suddenly declared that we would have certainly beaten Spain if only he had been there. Claims like that are much too straightforward.

Two hours before the semi-finals in Durban, Manni Draxler came up to me with tears in his eyes, apologising profusely. He had left my boots at the hotel in Centurion. They had toppled off a pile on the table and landed behind the drapes, and because I always wore turf boots during final training, no one had noticed. Drexler had another pair in his case, but I only played in boots I had already broken in at least four or five times. There was no way I could play in a brand-new pair. It was a no-go. In the end, Draxler soaked the boots in warm water for two hours, and they turned out okay. But it wasn't a good omen. We lost 1-0, a repeat of the Euros finale in Vienna. It was a close game, but Spain were as dominant as they had been two years earlier.

We thought we had learned from our mistakes and the tactics board might had been covered in the most beautiful ideas, but it changed nothing. We wanted to keep it tight at the back again, but be more active, exerting more pressure and pressing the ball much sooner. But that strategy only led to Spain being able to break through us more easily and to more problems. They managed the game relatively safely, without conceding too many shots on goal. Although we weren't entirely without chances — Toni Kroos had one good effort — the fact that we conceded from a corner was especially bitter. Losing two World Cup semi-finals in a row was very painful.

Returning to Germany on the back of a victory in the third-place playoff against Uruguay allowed us to keep faith, though. At that point, everyone knew that four years in football went by incredibly quickly: this generation would be given another chance. That kind of positive thinking was needed in order to get back up off the ground and keep running. A long season followed by a long tournament, a little time off, and the knowledge that the cycle would start all over again soon required that kind of optimism.

POLAND & UKRAINE 2012

DUE TO MY ANKLE INJURY, I LOST MY PERMANENT place on the team before the 2012 Euros. Löw had chosen Jérôme Boateng and Mats Hummels as his centre-halves for the tournament. 'There are two others now,' he told me. 'You're behind for now.' As a result, I developed self-doubts. 'Why won't you trust me anymore?' I asked. He pointed out that I had only just regained my fitness and that he was simply going to give preference to others. That hit me hard; I felt as if Jogi had lost faith in me.

After a few weeks, I tried to see things from his point of view, but I still didn't understand his decision. I slept badly. My head would buzz with questions at night. It took a while until I was ready to consider whether there might be an upside to the situation. I realised for the first time how reserve players must feel in all those tournaments I had played. It was a new, but crucial perspective that shed light on many things. Being confronted with new and sometimes uncomfortable truths aides a person in their development. Afterwards, I knew more about myself; specifically, I knew how I processed setbacks. I knew now how it felt not to be first choice. That period was among the most instructive, because it showed me even more clearly that football is a team sport. Not everything begins and ends with your own place in the first eleven. One can contribute in other ways, namely by supporting colleagues.

Over the course of the tournament in Poland, I noticed I was happy and motivated during training despite the disappointment of not playing. I wanted to prove myself, and that included the post-matchday session a day after a game, during which reserve players work through an extra programme which most players don't enjoy. The time on the bench reinforced my determination for a comeback. Even though I didn't play a single second and we were once more eliminated in the semi-finals, I found many arguments for preparing myself mentally and physically for the upcoming season.

After the defeat to Italy, Jogi was a nervous wreck. I think it was the first time in all those years that he doubted the squad and was no longer sure if things could continue this way. Everyone was downcast and we had hit rock bottom. When DFB president Wolfgang Niersbach gave a closing address at the hotel, Jogi simply stared at his plate. I can imagine that the thought of resignation had crossed his mind. But then, Niersbach said in a loud, clear voice that the 'project' would be continued with Löw as manager, that we would keep walking the path together despite all criticism, and that we would defy this setback. Löw didn't stir. I think that ultimately the association's trust in him and his trust in the squad convinced him to keep going. A few things needed changing, though. The way we had conducted ourselves as a team in 2012 had not been good enough.

In my mind, the growing rivalry between the Bayern and Dortmund camps wasn't even the biggest issue. We had many individualists on the team who all wanted the limelight, but not everybody got that chance and our team spirit was the victim. In retrospect, we needed to experience these conflicts in order to understand the importance of remaining whole as a squad.

BRAZIL 2014

I WAS DESPERATE TO PROVE TO MYSELF AND everyone else that I was able to return to the starting XI. The challenge to play a World Cup in South America and perhaps be the first European team to win there was just too alluring. Bayern and Dortmund's continental success had increased the rivalry for permanent international places. Things went back and forth during the qualifiers: sometimes, I played alongside Jérôme Boateng, sometimes Mats Hummels did. Mats and I never had issues on a personal level. It is important to accept that the team can win without you, and to be there for your colleagues despite any personal frustration over sitting on the bench. I always supported the squad and demanded the same of my teammates whenever I was picked. That's vital in any side, but there were some who hadn't understood that before the tournament began. There were moments during the qualifiers when individual players put their ego above the collective good and sulked when they didn't make the line-up.

On the brink of his 100th cap in September 2013, Philipp Lahm had a few choice words for the squad in agreement with the team council. During the run-up to the World Cup, the explicit aim was for everyone to get along better than in the past. The battles between Bayern and Dortmund had done damage to the atmosphere. Players from both clubs wanted to win big titles, titles that might be crucial to someone's career, so the rivalry was fierce and it couldn't just be turned off during the international break. We tried to solve these problems while planning and preparing the composition of Campo Bahia, our camp during the tournament. It wasn't possible just to put all Dortmund players into one room and all Bayern players into another and hope it would work. After the 2012 Euros, it was clear to many that these eight weeks in Brazil had to be a particularly special time. We needed to leave all prejudices at home and to work hard to actually get to know our teammates.

In the end, Oliver Bierhoff appointed four house captains: Philipp Lahm, Bastian Schweinsteiger, Miroslav Klose, and me. We were to allocate the rest of the squad to the bungalows at random in order to create new bonds and strengthen the team spirit. We applied a bit of a strategy — 'I'll take this one, you the other' — which resulted in interesting mixes that would later prove important. While rivalries are normal, they can be poison for a team, but the particular structure within the bungalows removed that problem. It was what this World Cup needed. Before, things had been in order, broadly speaking, but not to the point where people were ready to go through hell for each other. Bierhoff warned us that in Brazil, not everything would necessarily meet German standards, but at the same time, he raved about the extraordinary atmosphere. We thought it was going to be amazing.

The training camp in South Tyrol didn't get off to the best start, though. The weather was lousy, and we were all in low spirits after the touring car driver Pascal Wehrlein, with my defensive colleague Benedikt Höwedes in the passenger seat, hit a spectator and a marshal with his vehicle. The spectator, a tourist from Thuringia, was gravely injured. Benedikt was in a state of shock, but as a team, we didn't let ourselves be led astray. Every night, Lukas Podolski, Tim Wiese, and I visited the hotel's event sauna, big enough to fit fifty people. The reigning world sauna champions actually staged their shows here. They would dress up as Native Americans, Spider-Man, or the Phantom of the Opera. I had never seen anything like it. The three of us came up with the idea to add a note to the daily schedule.

'Mandatory team event! Meet at the sauna at 9pm. Motto: Sweating for success, in anticipation of the conditions in Brazil.'

It was a crackpot idea, but it worked. We all crammed ourselves in, the lights went out, and there followed a twelve-minute laser show. It was one of those small, seemingly incidental incidents that served to strengthen team spirit.

Prior to the tournament, Manuel Neuer, Philipp Lahm, Bastian Schweinsteiger, and Sami Khedira were not quite fit, which created some doubt. 'Let's start small,' we said. 'Think small. We'll have to survive the group phase first.' The biggest issue for me personally was Philipp Lahm playing in midfield and the ramifications that might have on the defence. It was Jogi's greatest concern, too; we talked about it a lot. During a conversation in Düsseldorf, before we were due to depart for Brazil, he asked me whether I could imagine playing with four centre-halves. Löw himself felt quite sure on the matter, but he wanted my opinion, as well as on the slightly reckless idea of shifting the right-footed Benedikt Höwedes to the left. For Benny, suddenly having the entire pitch on his right after having spent his whole life on the other side was a mammoth task. Our job was to support him as much as possible, to give him the right kind of passes that could be moved up the field. It probably wouldn't go completely without a hitch, but he played almost flawlessly and was one of the World Cup's great discoveries.

Playing a tournament with four centre-halves was a first, of course, and didn't represent the ideal line-up, either. But Jogi urgently needed Lahm in the centre, because Sami and Bastian would not be fit for the opener against Portugal. The four in defence were skilled players and knew how to build our game from the back. In addition, the set-up would give us a great advantage in the air at set-pieces. We would start out this way to create stability, then take it from there. There was also a slight change in midfield: Jogi Löw shifted from the familiar 4-2-3-1 to a 4-3-3. Three people in front of the defence was an elegant solution to an old problem: apart from Christoph Kramer, there was no real defensive midfielder in the squad. By adding a man in the centre, Löw had adapted to the conditions in Brazil. We wanted to keep it tight at the back and allow fewer gaps. As far as Mesut was concerned, his new position on the left of a front three certainly wasn't his favourite; he was more comfortable in a more central spot or on the other side, from where he could drift inwards. But Thomas Müller was set on the right, so Löw and the team needed Mesut on the left. 'We'll need him,' was Löw's constant mantra.

Mesut's biggest job was to use his exceptional technique to maintain possession and to support Benny Höwedes on the left, both defensively and offensively. We were not to lose possession on this side, because the switch in play was supposed to be initiated from here. Accepting and taking on this task was a big step. It came as a surprise to many, but it was also one of the many keys to our success. There were 23 of us, and each one had a role of his own; we could never have made it if Mesut had said he didn't fancy playing that position. He sacrificed himself for the team and that sent a strong signal to the rest of the group that individual interests weren't a priority.

Jogi had very clear ideas about how to approach an opponent. When it came to defending, technically advanced players in particular benefited from these precise instructions. The squad had always been aware of Mesut's capabilities, like the fact that he could draw opposition players towards him by making runs beyond the defensive line. He was world class. The distances he covered, especially at pace, were extraordinary. At top speed, he did two kilometres in a game; only a few others managed the same. Jogi kept stressing that: he wanted us to know how much work Mesut was doing, how high his intensity levels were, and how many sprints he did. Löw praised players he picked for things that might have been overlooked and lauded those he didn't for their work in training. He made everyone feel important; it was a masterpiece in coaching. For me, it was nice to know that Jogi trusted me again after I hadn't played at all during the prior tournament.

Facing Portugal and Cristiano Ronaldo in our opening game didn't scare us. We had beaten them in 2006, 2007 and 2012; they didn't like playing us. Nevertheless, we travelled to Brazil with some trepidation. A system with four centre-halves, a camp that probably hadn't been finished yet, long trips, the unfamiliar climate; Jogi knew he had to prepare the squad for unknown factors. It was all the more important for him to involve the team in his decisions early on. A few members of the coaching staff made the journey to the camp three days before us. Their feedback was not encouraging. 'No chance. They're never going to be finished in time.' Completely straight faced, Manuel Neuer replied, 'No problem, I've always wanted to camp on the beach.'

People like that are essential in those situations: on the pitch, things are never predictable, and unexpected problems are never far away. To us, Brazil was uncharted territory. The long trips were a little unusual, starting with the ferry we had to keep taking on the way to the airport. The Brazilian people are enthralled by the game, so they were immensely open and friendly towards us, with the exception of the time we played their team. The rest of the time, though, they were very eager to help and grateful to host the World Cup. Their joy was infectious. During the three days before we arrived, incredible work was done to make everything look smart. Fit for a team of world champions. When we finally got there, we were delighted: we were going to sleep in houses with living rooms that faced the beach and eat under the stars. My house discovered the ping-pong table on our very first day, and we played round robin, barefoot in forty-degree heat. After five or ten minutes of non-stop roaring, there were fifteen of us crowded around the table. The result was lots of fun and lots of blisters on everyone's feet. We went into first training with a handicap, but it didn't matter; no one wanted to stop.

Oliver Bierhoff hadn't wanted a regular hotel with fifty rooms in a row, but rather to create a special atmosphere, the perfect combination of holiday feeling and open-air work space. And he did. Every relative who came to visit was amazed by what they found. The first time Oliver had been on site a year before the start of the tournament, when there had been nothing there, he had sensed what was possible. There had been a lot of resistance, and he had been forced to tear down many walls, but he believed in his vision and made it a reality. As warden of the base, if you will, his share in our eventual success was immense: the intangibles released by the camp had won us the title. It's difficult to describe, but returning after each game to recharge and head back out was a real joy. Usually, base camps are quite boring — sitting in a small room with a laptop, trying not to succumb to cabin fever — but Campo Bahia had an enchanting effect on us from the start. Internally, Bierhoff was an anchor of calm and also a kind of shield for the coaching staff. He had a good sense for timing and was often on hand to say the right thing, be it praising the team or assessing a win. He didn't do it to take centre stage but to serve the cause.

Bierhoff was also indispensable to the team council where the coordination of marketing operations was concerned, acting as a point of contact for us. Because the team's popularity had soared since 2004, sponsors were clamouring for us, but things had never got out of hand. Everything was well regulated. Of course, there was a lot of money involved, both for the team and the association. Bierhoff had insisted everything be divided up fairly, so that the stars wouldn't be the only ones making a profit. It shouldn't be underestimated how important this set-up was to the team structure. Back then, salaries had usually been staggered according to minutes played, which had led to frequent arguments. In Brazil, however, every place on the team was considered the same for the benefit of the collective. It was good that reserve players were also rewarded for their work. Every day, Löw praised those who weren't being used and emphasised the fact that they too were responsible for our performances. Time and again, he catered to their needs, paying them attention in front of the others. He virtually neglected the first eleven.

The approach stood out. There are always two or three newbies on a team who are simply glad to be there, but there are also five or six who think they should be playing and aren't quite as happy with their reserve status. In Brazil, we were motivated by the idea that we had to get through it all together. No longer were there whispers of negativity. Instead, people said they were sure a good set of players would make the team. There was a desire to keep an open mind about these things, because we knew that our colleagues were just as good. Everyone bore responsibility for the greater good, and everyone accepted the others as fully fledged members of the group. Things had been very different at the Euros, but now, everything clicked. It worked.

What was new was the fact that, as experienced players, Philipp Lahm and I were being included in the tactical preparations. The coaching staff wanted us to give feedback on both scouting results and the game plan beforehand, so they could make sure everything would make sense to the rest of the squad. 'We want your input and your trust,' they said. 'Are we picking the right people? Is this really the system we'll want to play? Will that come across properly on the pitch?' The work done by Urs Siegenthaler's team was excellent. Ultimately, it was more about a discussion with the manager, about a healthy exchange of opinions. Giving more responsibility to two players who had been around for a while and were challenging each other consistently wasn't a bad idea. The game plan wasn't supposed to overwhelm the squad. A certain amount of creative freedom on the ball is vital, but without it, a proper structure is essential.

How did we want to build up our game from the back? How did we want to work our way into midfield and the final third? How did we want to organise ourselves at the back when we were in possession? How did we cover each other? How would we begin our attacks?

There were a lot of variations. Which zones did we want to attack? Which players did we want to attack, and when? Should we block the front completely? Should we let the opposing team build up their game along the wings? Should we allow them to move the ball forward and then only start pressing from midfield?

These were the kind of subtleties that needed refinement. We had met Portugal before, and so we knew that we could prepare as much as we wanted for someone like Cristiano Ronaldo. But we were also aware that such a world-class player was able to adapt to a game and act completely differently in a specific moment than he had done in the scouting videos. But it's important to occupy oneself with the job, to consider, and to both take on and take away a lot of information. The squad joined in. Hansi Flick kept calling on individual players, too. 'Let's take another look at those set pieces,' he would say. 'Look at that again. See, if this happens, the ball comes from over there.' They wouldn't leave us alone, in a good way.

Usually, players return to their rooms after official team meetings; they were used to having most things done for them, including thinking and reasoning. At Camp Bahia, though, we were constantly kept on our toes. Personal responsibility was a key phrase from the beginning. There were six people to a house. Whether they liked each other or not, we were responsible for making it work. The coaching staff enforced the rule that everyone was to tend to things by themselves; how the warm-up would go, for example, or how to organise set pieces. There was a lot of value placed on the latter. In the past, we had somewhat neglected set pieces: for a long time, Jogi Löw's priorities had been elsewhere. Generally, set-piece training tends to be tedious: while seven people get to be involved in the action, the other three stand in the back, scratching their balls. No one really wants to do the exercise properly, as they think the situation will develop differently during a game anyway. Training set pieces properly, with the necessary force and precision, takes time and energy.

In South Tyrol, however, Hansi Flick had something else in mind. There was to be two teams, and each team would take three corners and three set pieces each. If the ball was cleared by the defending team it remained live, which meant play was to continue on a tight pitch with two goals and a scoring system. We were never allowed to switch off. Over time, this approach gave rise to a proper competitive atmosphere. We came up with all kinds of versions, including some wild ideas that didn't work in the end, like Thomas Müller's famous stumbled dummy in the build-up to a free-kick against Algeria. He had copied it from the penalty shootout between Afghanistan and the Maldives. Most of the time, the first team played the reserves, which meant that over the course of the tournament, the starting XI became more and more attuned to each other and developed sequences that actually benefited the team during a game. Not just because the choreography patterns had become second nature, but because there was the conviction that if one stood in an exact spot, the ball would land precisely where it was supposed to. There was a developing trust.

The set pieces quickly revealed the advantage of having four centre-halves. We had a presence in the box, both in the defence and the attack, with many dangerous players. It paid off; five goals were created from corners or free-kicks. When it came to defending set pieces, we wanted to learn from past mistakes. Fundamentally, we stuck with a zonal defence, meaning the four players with the most aerial power positioned themselves in the risk zones, independent of the opposition players. Manuel Neuer felt most at ease with this approach; he didn't want a teammate on the post, let alone on the line. The disadvantage with this system, as we had learned against Spain during the 2010 World Cup semi-final, is that it allows the opponent a free run in the box. That's the worst thing for a defence: a zonal system leaves defenders static, giving forwards the advantage of a running-jump, and that's exactly how Puyol had scored the only goal in Durban. Together, we reflected on how to improve.

The solution was to play both in the space and close to the man. The four tallest were to mark the space, aided by three others, who obstructed the opposition's path and robbed them of any advantage they would have had with unobstructed runs. Thanks to Pep Guardiola, Manuel Neuer was familiar with a similar version of this tactic and led our approach with his own ideas, but everyone had to contribute, of course, especially the forwards, who now had to cope with a giant group of defenders during set pieces.

From our point of view, there would have been no point in setting up three marionettes – we needed players who would get close to the man and weren't afraid of getting hurt. Thomas Müller, for instance, could be a pain in the neck all day; he didn't mind if things got a little rough. It was reassuring to know that there was someone who kept opposition attackers busy, who didn't just let them pass. We felt very much at ease in this system; so much so that over the course of the entire tournament, we didn't concede a single goal from a set piece.

We had an incredible start against Portugal. 4-0, with three Müller goals. The next day, I said in an interview that we now had to 'bring it home'. I couldn't have been all there; it was the adrenaline and exhilaration talking after all the worries beforehand. It was far too early to be making statements like that. A lot can happen during a tournament. On the other hand, it was a sign of our growing self-confidence: since 2004, we had always made it to the finals or at least the semi-finals, and we wanted to keep that up. Just how long that journey was going to be became clear during the 2-2 draw against Ghana. It was a chaotic, back-

and-forth game. It could have just as easily finished 5-5, and Ghana had enough counter-attacking opportunities to beat us. Barely anything was left of all the tricks we had thought up for the Portugal game. There was a complete lack of stability.

There are days when the small things aren't quite right, and sometimes, those small things end up multiplying out of control. The insecurity became contagious, like a virus. My first few passes didn't quite reach their destination, and I couldn't assert myself in tackles. It was my 100th cap and my first wedding anniversary to boot, so I was charged with positive energy, but I had a bad feeling on the pitch. To top it all off, it was incredibly hot and humid in Fortaleza, not our kind of weather at all. Ghana were touch-tight: very strong physically, very close to the man, and very awkward to play.

It was obvious: they wanted to show everyone who they were, that they were someone in this World Cup, too. Every now and then, there are teams who manage to pull off *the* performance, and Ghana came very close. That's what makes football what it is: nothing is certain. We were struggling terribly. We weren't infallible, and anyway, anyone could have a bad day as an individual. As a team, we had to cope with the situation and play our way out of trouble. Afterwards, the most important message for us was that when push came to shove, we were still capable of responding with force. Miro Klose had scored the late equaliser after a corner. It was a good signal, a sense of certainty that we had enough quality in the squad to achieve a good result, even if we played dreadfully, were continually off the pace, and didn't really create many chances.

Still, the draw caused expectations to be lowered. We had again tumbled from the very top, almost all the way to the bottom. If the tournament was the ocean, this was the trough of our wave. We yearned for calm waters and blue skies, but often the sea was restless under a thunderstorm. It happened a lot, and most of the time, that was a good thing: the adversity sharpened our senses and our defences. We needed at least a draw in our third group match, so we were extremely focused before kick-off against the US. The reunion with Jürgen Klinsmann in Recife was emotional. He had been the inspiration for this team, the initial spark. It had been he who had normalised giving young players a chance very early on, and ten years later, we were still benefitting from the changes he had brought about. Now, though, he was sitting on the other bench.

Due to torrential rains the night before, we hadn't been allowed to train in the stadium, and only got to warm-up on the sidelines. In the end, however, the pitch was fine. Our confidence was back, too. With Schweinsteiger in midfield instead of Khedira, as well as Lahm and Kroos, we were very calm and confident on the ball. Müller's goal came from a corner, after the US goalkeeper had only managed to swat away my header. Afterwards, the Bayern camp engaged in a bit of politics. Everyone was praising Schweini, who had indeed played very well in his first full game, and subsequently, Sami was slightly miffed. He had fought his way back after his ligament rupture and had got back to fitness in the nick of time, but instead of him playing in the centre, it had been Lahm, the normal right-back.

Sami was an incredible bloke and crucial to the team, but

sometimes he was a little negative. There are people who harvest an immense amount of energy from feeling hard done by, and it was this attitude which motivated him (granted, within reason). The rat race was on. Everyone had their own angle and their own reason to believe in their value to the side. No problem. Where the team as a whole was concerned, the most important thing was for all key players to be fit in time for the knockout games and to be willing to play. Everyone was there, everyone was available, and Löw was spoilt for choice. Who had which strengths? Who was more important to the team at that point? Löw didn't care one bit about inter-club bickering or whatever the papers were saying. He was above the little things. He used the camp's remoteness to reflect properly and make decisions that were completely in the team's interest without worrying about individual sensitivities. He would isolate himself entirely and was fully independent.

Then came Algeria. Where the course of the game was concerned, we were faced with another Ghana, only much more dramatic. We escaped a national sporting catastrophe by the skin of our teeth. Eliminated in the round of sixteen by Algeria? That would have been the worst World Cup of any German team ever. Fortunately, we weren't thinking quite as far ahead during the match. The idea didn't form in the back of our minds, which was lucky. Otherwise, the fear would have probably paralysed us altogether. It did feel similar to the Ghana game, though. When in possession, we were lax, erratic, and wasteful. Everyone was battling with themselves. We didn't infiltrate the final third properly and struggled to push forward into the attacking zones.

Algeria were so quick on their feet, they covered so much of the space in their own half, and our game was too slow to create any overloads in the right areas.

They were surprisingly good. That is always the greatest danger when it comes to teams like this: there are always unfamiliar players in their side, so they're a much harder opponent to prepare for. Suddenly, it become clear how quick and aggressive Algeria were. They would lay the ball off and immediately make runs behind our defence, where there was an enormous amount of room behind our high line. They had a clear plan, and we didn't manage to protect the ball or prevent their counter-attacks. We couldn't cope. With virtually every attack, Algeria managed to pose a threat to our goal; it was extremely unpleasant. Frankly, we could count ourselves lucky to have a sweeper 'keeper.

Manuel Neuer was known for his ability to read the game and anticipate dangerous situations, but never before had it been necessary to depend on that quite so often. He was world class. Without him, we would have struggled to advance into the next round. The goalless draw at half-time almost felt like success and it took until long into the second half for us to re-emerge. Algeria's stamina was diminishing, and we finally began to look stronger. After a hundred caps, one appreciates how quickly a game can turn.

As a footballer, that knowledge is ingrained: as poor as that last move was, the next one might be better. Not allowing oneself to be rattled by mistakes is a battle. There are players who absolutely cannot cope with situations like that and as a result do nothing but play safe, trying to avoid mistakes. Everyone reacts differently, but the impulse not to take another risk, to reduce oneself to the basics, is a good start. Our game was guided by pragmatism. *What's the priority right now? A diagonal ball across fifty metres and a dream pass into my teammate's path? Or is it more important to be in possession and regain security?* We had to go on, even if for eighty minutes, it didn't look like we were winning. Thinking like that helps. It's a character test.

Thanks to our maturity, our class, and our physique, we rediscovered our true selves. In extra time, we struck the decisive blows, even though it took a while for André Schürrle and Mesut Özil to score. It was that Bayern mentality to an extent: we knew that whatever happened, we would end the game on top — we would win the Cup. In the end, we were incredibly proud to have made it into the next round and to have delivered for Germany. It was the only thought I had after 120 minutes. I was at the limit, both physically and mentally. I high-fived everyone, thanked the fans, and dragged myself into the tunnel.

German broadcaster ZDF had requested other players for the live interview, but they hadn't been able to make it. Suddenly, press officer Uli Voigt appeared by my side. 'Right here,' he said. I was soaked in sweat and completely shattered. 'Yeah, okay.' The lights came on. Usually, the first question tends to be a softball, designed to let players talk. *Usually.* But Boris Büchler wanted to get straight to the point, the point being that things couldn't continue this way. 'What made the German game so cumbersome and vulnerable?'

Here we go. 'I couldn't care less,' I replied. I don't know what got into me; I just wanted to block all the negatives out and not allow any of them near me, much less confess to any kind of vulnerability within the side. After all, once those were voiced, they would be registered by others and had the potential to grow larger and larger. I wanted to nip that in the bud, but Büchler wouldn't let up.

'But that can't be the standard you had aimed for beforehand,' he persisted. 'You must be aware that there will have to be an improvement in the quarter-finals.'

'What is it you want from me here?' I shot back. 'What do you want from me when the game has only just finished? I don't get it.' I refused to have that happy moment stolen from me, but I couldn't seem to find the words for it. Usually, I would embellish and outline everything, considering every single sentence carefully, but my rejection of any kind of criticism erupted unchecked, allowing my emotions to spill out. Büchler still wasn't satisfied. 'First, let me congratulate you and then ask why things didn't go according to plan with regards to defending and transitioning today.'

'Do you think the last sixteen's a carnival or what? They made our life really difficult over two hours. We fought until the end and came out on top, especially during extra time. It was a proper up and down. We showed courage. Yes, we allowed a lot of chances, but we still kept a clean sheet. And what's more, in the end, we deserved to win. As for everything else, I'll be spending three days in an ice bath, and then we'll take it from there.'

I didn't normally say things like that. I had overheated; my synapses were no longer working. Eventually, I realised this myself, which is why I thought of the ice bath: I had to cool off, keep a cool head. On the plane, the squad gave me feedback. 'Oh, that's going to become of one those legendary post-match interviews,' Mats Hummels said, laughing. I think many of them approved of the fact that we had defended ourselves against all the criticism. I think there is nothing wrong with resolving these things out in the open. We were quick to bury the rest of the matter. I never watched that match again. I'm sure we did analysis in the days after, but I don't remember any of it. It's been erased from my mind. Our joy at progressing to the next round surpassed any negatives encountered on the journey. Dealing with a situation like this, having barely avoided elimination, you have to compartmentalise, almost play dumb at times.

What is this really about? We've reached the next round; we have a world-class 'keeper; we got our act together. We'll be more familiar with the next team, gear ourselves up properly, and play a better game. We can't act like this anymore. Playing another wild game like this won't work; we'll have to do better. We're growing. We're learning.

I think if everything only ever goes smoothly during a tournament, you'll eventually get caught out. In Brazil, we never slackened; we couldn't afford to. In retrospect, Ghana and Algeria were our critical moments. Both times, we had reached a dead end and that should have been it. After the previous tournaments, we had gained a reputation as a pretty, but mentally fragile side, one with a tendency to break apart quickly when things weren't going the way we wanted. We had been lugging around this baggage, but finally managed to get rid of it in Brazil. We had proven to ourselves that we were capable of asserting our game on less than good days, too. Meanwhile, Spain and Italy, our nemeses from the previous four competitions, had been eliminated already. Psychologically, that was crucial for us. We felt like the team of the moment, like we stood a real chance. Some kind of force had to be at work. It was meant to be.

During tournaments, every match is played as a reaction to the one before. The encounter with Algeria had convinced Löw that we were in need of a new impulse. After Shkodran Mustafi got injured in Porto Alegre, he had brought on Sami Khedira twenty minutes before the end of regular time and shifted Lahm to his traditional position at right-back. According to Löw, that was also where Lahm should play in the quarter-finals against France. Mats Hummels, who had been absent in Porto Alegre due to illness, was back in the starting line-up, and Jérôme Boateng remained at centre-half, which meant that I was out. The night before the game, Löw asked me into his hotel room to tell me the news, and because the line-up wasn't going to be announced until the next day, I couldn't talk to anyone about it.

I couldn't sleep all night, something that was never usually a problem for me. Many players bring their own pillow for hotel stays, or even a specific mattress. Others are so agitated that they take sleeping pills. I had always been able to switch off properly before a tournament in order to recover, no matter the bed or pillow, which made this phenomenon all the worse. I didn't manage to get a single second's sleep. *Why me? If you're out now, will the others think you're not good enough? Why can't you get over this?* I didn't have any answers, only questions, questions that kept repeating themselves. It was as if I was riding a merry-go-round and couldn't get off. A fever dream, but I was fully conscious. The next morning, I was all over the place, completely down and exhausted at breakfast.

You're not playing another game. Not another second. Your World Cup's over. It was wearing me down. Kick-off was at one o'clock in the afternoon, the hottest time of the tournament's hottest day. Just under thirty degrees. I was so out of it, I'm not sure I could have played at all if someone had got injured. I was virtually useless. It floored me, so much so that I was bedridden for a while after the game, but I don't think anyone noticed. Using the bit of energy I had left, I wanted to support the team as best I could, carrying water on the sidelines, for example. I was determined for my personal situation to have no effect on the others.

That was important to me. I know what it's like when individuals, thinking they ought to be playing, get angry and let others know. It's the worst. For instance, you notice at once whether someone wishes you good luck before a game and whether they actually mean it. On no account did I want my frustration to infect others. The World Cup wasn't won on the pitch alone but on the bench, too. At the end of the day, it was about Germany, and that took priority over Jogi's decision, which was probably only prudent again, anyway. Eventually, I realised he was doing everything right. Against France in the Maracaná – a stadium Thomas Müller described as a smokehouse – both teams became exhausted very quickly, and so the only question left to answer was who would get the first goal. Luck was on our side: Mats Hummels scored with a header from a corner, and Manuel Neuer had another excellent day. There are players who make just that bit of a difference; in Manuel's case, it was the difference between us going home or lifting the World Cup. My guess is that, in those temperatures, we could have only survived against a European team, anyway. Over the last ten, fifteen minutes, everyone was dead on their feet. After the match, I swapped shirts with Laurent Koscielny, who despite already being France's best centre-half back then, hadn't played much over the course of the tournament and had only been brought on late against us. He deserved to play even more than I did. *At least you're not alone.*

For the third time in a row, Germany had made into the semi-finals of a World Cup, and we were proud of our consistency. Other countries would have been satisfied at this point, but how much was it really worth without taking home the trophy? More than once, we had not quite made it to the top. After all the climbing we had done, we were forced to turn around just before reaching the peak. Twice, we had been eliminated in the semi-finals, and despite coming third in the end and going home relatively happy, we were desperate to avoid a repeat. We were determined to settle for nothing less than ultimate success in Brazil.

Our situation was similar to Italy's before the semi-finals in Dortmund eight years earlier. This wasn't just going to be a match against eleven Brazilians but against an entire country. We were taking on the World Cup's script. We knew that in order to make the final, we had to play beyond our standards in Belo Horizonte. Before the tournament, Jogi Löw had talked of 'primal forces' that needed vanquishing. We couldn't allow ourselves to be knocked off our stride by this atmosphere, created by two hundred million exhilarated people. *If we make it, if we knock out the hosts, then we'll win the tournament. Then we'll have the right to take home that trophy.*

Unlike the match against Spain in South Africa, we wanted to attack straight away, with speed, to force Brazil into playing direct from the back and into our defence's hands. Jogi's instruction was to press high, again and again. As a team, it was easier for us attack early and high up rather than standing on the halfway line. If you surrender the first fifty metres, it can be tricky to find the necessary aggression to recover the ball in time. Compared to 2010, the quality of individual players and the overall quality of the squad had increased considerably, which had an immediate effect on our game and our confidence. We were no longer that team who waited for a situation and only resorted to counter-attacks three or four times during a match. We were too eager for possession to be cautious. With Mesut playing on the left, we had four classic midfielders on the pitch who knew how to express themselves on the ball. We had the players needed to dominate possession and the opponent.

Mentally, we were bracing ourselves for a very rough match. Jogi was incredibly aggressive during the team meeting after Luiz Felipe Scolari had announced that his side would polish us off. He printed off the article with Scolari's quotes and pinned it onto the wall in the meeting room. 'He's just whistling in the dark,' he said. 'They're scared of us. They're only pretending to be this confident, because they know we can beat them in their own country.' By the end, his voice had risen to a scream. 'Lads, they're just whistling in the dark!' Löw was to be proven right;

Brazil buckled under the pressure. Thiago Silva was suspended and Neymar injured.

Before kick-off, they commemorated their superstar in a video message with lots of pathos and tears, overdoing it entirely. We delivered our performance on the pitch, cool as you like. Müller opened proceedings with a set-piece.

2-0. 3-0. 4-0. 5-0. The way the midfield constructed those goals was from another planet. Sami ran like a madman. We reserves felt like organ pipes on the bench: up, down, up, down; we might as well have been on the pitch. It was our job to energise the team from the sidelines. After a while, we took to staring at each other. 'No way. This can't be true. We must be dreaming.' By half-time, the stadium was in shock. Immeasurable disappointment in the stands turned into scorn and derision. It was brutal. Nothing like that will ever happen again.

At half-time, Mats was ailing, and Jogi turned to face me. My time had come. By that point, I had already put the tournament behind me in my mind. As a centre-half, if you're not in the first eleven, you're not playing. I thought I wouldn't play another minute: usually, three offensive players would have been subbed on. Receiving another chance against the odds felt divine. I could tell that Jogi was also glad he could reward me one more time for my conduct in training and on the bench. 'You're coming on, and you'll do it the way you always do.' Hearing him say that was a wonderful moment; his trust in me had not disappeared.

During the break, Jogi urged us to maintain our focus. After all, we had first-hand knowledge of what couple happen if we didn't. A few months previously, we had been 4-0 up during a qualifier against Sweden, only to end up drawing four-all. The fact that the momentum could pivot that quickly was a warning for us. A single goal, and the mood could turn. After Sweden, there had been a hailstorm of criticism, but the game had been educational. It became part of this team's history. Fortunately, Manuel Neuer was virtually unbeatable in Belo Horizonte. He made a number of excellent saves when Brazil came close to consolation goals. At that level of the game, irrespective of the score or circumstances, it's impossible to subdue the opposition entirely, so you need a 'keeper like this behind you, one who assures you that even if an opposition player gets through on goal, nothing would happen; Manuel sorted things for us. He was hugely frustrated about conceding in the last minute, as was Jérôme; it was indicative of our mentality. 7-1 against Brazil, a historic win. For a while, it felt as if we were already world champions. Fortunately, there wasn't too much time to ponder, and we quickly returned back to Earth.

No, no, no. This won't mean anything if we don't complete it now. If we don't win that trophy, we'll make an absolute spectacle of ourselves. Which was true — if we didn't win the World Cup after beating the hosts 7-1, then it would be a huge let-down. I don't even want to imagine what would have happened had we not made it past the finish line. I managed to block out those heavy thoughts about this being my last World Cup and about our last chance to prove that we were the golden generation. Too much musing over such things, over the consequences of failure, and we wouldn't have made it. It's okay to acknowledge the tension. There needs to be a certain level of respect, and there is nothing wrong with allowing yourself to feel some fear. But you have to know how to cope with it. That was crucial. In the run-up to the final, we were absolutely convinced of our own abilities. We thought we would walk our own path, no matter how the game developed.

Following the semi-finals, all the media criticism · turned to praise, and it came from all directions. We only had ARD and ZDF in the camp, but both channels were showing footage of the mood in Germany. We never took it for granted, but made it plain to ourselves time and again what exactly that meant. That German catchphrase, 'The whole country's behind you,' had finally arrived in Brazil. Seeing the celebrations after the goals gave you instant goosebumps. The energy was palpable, even from thousands of kilometres away. Interestingly, dealing with praise and affection can sometimes be more difficult than dealing with criticism. All the world telling us we were the best and we would win easily buzzed in our ears, but it was quickly overshadowed by a different tune. *One more game.* The last game. Another round of 90 or 120 minutes. No matter who gets injured, no matter who needs to come off, we would deal with it all, because it just meant that someone else would play in their place. Oliver Bierhoff had something else up his sleeve. 'We've been together for so long,' he said. 'It's written somewhere that we'll win this thing. We'll make it. If we want it as one, we'll make it as one.'

When we left the camp for the last time, there was a sense of melancholy among the squad. On the ferry, I stood as I always did next to Benny Höwedes, and the two of us paused, because we knew we would never come back to this place. This beautiful time would never return. If anyone thought that during the two days we spent in a Rio hotel before the final, we might lose the solidarity we had gained in the camp, they were wrong. We kept our bunker mentality. The general mood in Brazil had shifted in our favour. People had been angry with us at first, but then, the fear of an even greater catastrophe arose: arch-enemies Argentina wining the World Cup in the Maracanã. *Anything* but that. From a Brazilian standpoint, it would definitely be better if we won. We managed to take that momentum with us into the match. The fact that we already knew the ground from our win over France was also an advantage. Little things like that are important to footballers.

Which item of clothing do I put on first? Which manoeuvre works, what will I be doing again next time? Who's sitting next to me to make me feel comfortable?

The familiarity of certain sequences allows you to breathe more calmly. One might call it superstition, or maybe routine. Humans tend to hold on to whatever they know: things, methods, other people. In my case, it was socks: left before right. It was also important to me lay out all my stuff beforehand, like sock tape. I was very fussy that way. I didn't, for instance, want to have to sprint through the dressing room after the warm-up to grab something I had left behind. What was more, I had a clear order for the stretching exercises with which I prepared for the match at the hotel. After the team meeting, we spent the last hour before departure in our rooms, where I began my prep. It was a fixed programme designed to tune the body, accompanied by music.

Over the course of the tournament, I had always been next to Philipp Lahm in the dressing and saw just how quietly he sat there before kick-off. It told me that there wouldn't be a problem, that he would play as he always did. Substituting Mats against Brazil had been a precautionary measure, and he was back at a hundred percent for the final. But I wondered what might happen. Perhaps we would be in the lead just before the end and need someone to make one last header. That's how I pictured it. And sometimes, things happen the way you've pictured them. Needless to say, when it came to the game itself, the semi-finals against Brazil wouldn't be beaten: it had almost been too easy. I was worried that things would be a lot trickier against Argentina. And we were off to a poor start, too. Shortly before kick-off, Sami Khedira had to withdraw because of injury. He was replaced by Christoph Kramer, who had barely started a single international in his life. Fifteen minutes into the game, Kramer went down, knocked unconscious by Ezequiel Garay. When he came off, Christoph didn't know where he was. He was replaced by André Schürrle, and Mesut shifted into the centre as number ten.

Two adjustments in the first few minutes that completely changed the team structure, and in a World Cup final too. Other teams would have struggled. Not this team, though. We took it in our stride. Argentina, however, had the better chances. If we're being honest, they even had really good chances. At one point during the first half, a stray Toni Kroos header fell straight into the path of Gonzalo Higuaín, through on goal and with only

Manuel Neuer to beat. He took a shot — and missed. On the bench, Khedira and I exchanged looks. We both had the same thought. *They're not scoring against us today. They won't manage to.* Around half-time, we are all thinking it. *They can play for another five hours, but they won't get the ball behind that line. This is our day, no matter what happens.*

The cards were stacked against us, but we were so determined that the pure football aspect took a backseat. For years, it was said that we were superior, that we could sidestep anyone. But a side's true nature only becomes apparent on days their technical brilliance can't be converted. I learned that a team's essence, the invisible bond holding it together, is more important than the neatest low pass, the sleekest combination, or the most beautiful goal. In that final, we were only able to call upon a fraction of our true quality for a number of reasons. But we knew we were a great team, a crew of lads who were invested in the cause with all their hearts and feeling that so plainly really was exceptional. Those eight weeks were the time of our lives. During the second half of extra time, it was clear I wouldn't be deployed. Kevin Großkreutz was already standing by the touchline, ready to be brought on; he was supposed to be our third substitution. But then, Mario scored that goal. The most beautiful goal in the world. Kevin was ordered back onto the bench.

'Sit back down,' Jogi told him. It was my turn now, it had to be. There wasn't long to go, and we needed someone who would soar into the air at the back and head the ball away. We needed *me*. Fortunately, after 119 minutes, Jogi took a similar view. 'Put on your kit,' he said. 'The boys are spinning out there.' The energy on the bench was supernatural. 'You'll kill it!' they roared at me. My pulse was slightly higher than usual, I'll admit that. My chance to play in a World Cup Final after a tournament like this had been virtually zero, so playing three or four minutes was all the more wonderful in the end. A second after I had come on, I followed up on a Neuer clearance. In the stands, the German fans cried out. Never before had I received that much applause for a header. It was to be my only touch. We were already three minutes into stoppage-time at the end of extra time when Argentina were awarded a free-kick.

Deadly silence settled on the stadium. Messi took his time. *Just put it over, Messi. Don't put in a cross, just aim for the goal and miss. It's the best thing you could be doing now.*

And he did. It was time for us to get ready for... well, what? We didn't actually know quite what to do in that moment when the referee blew his whistle. What did you do when you were world champions? Before I knew it, I was lying under an enormous mound of people, wedged in between the rest of the squad. Someone's elbow was pressing into my throat; I could hardly breathe. Afterwards, my neck hurt from being embraced so vigorously by everyone. I still remember lifting Philipp Lahm into the air at one point. We were paying tribute to each other. My neck pains were the only thing bothering me. It hurt so badly, I needed treatment. 'Klaus, I'm done. My neck hurts like hell.' Something must have got dislocated. 'Klaus, I can't go on; I need to go inside. I can't feel my neck. It's over.'

I gave Mario Götze the tightest of hugs: I needed to show him that all the work he had undertaken beside our usual training had paid off. We had done hours and hours of yoga together, even here in Brazil whenever we felt the need. Extra care, extra physio therapy, extra sessions. Mario had taken up Neuro Athletic training for the World Cup, supervised by Lars Lienhard, where we would run into each other a lot. All that effort had paid off at the Maracanã, our year-long graft condensed into a single, enduring moment. Sharing this joy for a few minutes with every member of the team was the most moving part of the evening, perhaps even more than the win itself. On stage, trophy in hand, I still couldn't quite believe it. In the dressing room, FIFA representatives immediately locked the original back up in the Louis Vuitton case, leaving us to continue celebrating with a replica.

I found myself sitting next to Phillipp once more, shirt numbers sixteen and seventeen. We looked into each other's eyes, and there was the same question on both our lips. *What could possibly be next?* For ten years, we had run this marathon together and now it was over. There was something final about the situation. These thoughts only became firmly established over the next few days, but at the root, just a few minutes after the final whistle, we both knew that this was it. Angela Merkel joined us in the dressing room for a lovely group picture, and I had everyone sign my shirt. It was given to Paul Kalkbrenner in exchange for a £10,000 donation to my charitable foundation. We did the conga from one end of the mixed zone to the other, past hundreds of journalists, singing loudly. Nothing else needed to be said; we had already said it all. Now, it was time to enjoy our triumph. The journey back to the hotel was sensational. I sat down in the middle of the bus, already slightly drunk. Everyone was required to sing. Here was my chance put to use all those songs from my class outings in the Harz, so I belted out a few of those. The coaching staff were sitting at the front, quite controlled. We tried to bring Jogi out of his shell by signing 'Oh, dear Jogi, sing a song,' to the tune of *'Dornröschen war ein schönes Kind'*, a German nursery rhyme. But he wouldn't sing. All we got out of him was a wave, but that was enough to make the bus erupt in cheers.

It was superb. Completely exuberant, but peaceful. It was also the last time we as a team would be among ourselves. All by ourselves. At the hotel, there was a great big party: families, officials, sponsors, followers, actors, Rihanna; it was a riot. There were lots of people there who knew that today, this was the centre of the Earth, because these were the world champions, and there was the Cup. I got a lovely selfie with the trophy. The DJ was great, the alcohol levels were huge, and the dancing was uninhibited. I busted my slinky moves with the winners' medal wrapped around my forehead. It was fitting, but it no longer had much to do with us as people, which I thought was a pity.

I would have preferred a private celebration among the people with whom I had spent eight weeks, shedding blood and sweat. It was over too quickly; we didn't have time for adequate reflection. The flight back home, the fan park in Berlin, the party with our fans — we went from one vortex into the next, unable to block out the knowledge that there would be something else around the corner. Off on holiday, then back to our clubs, back to everyday life. When you're being screamed out of bed by your second baby at five or six in the morning, the World Cup is as far away as the Moon from the Earth.

My two sons didn't know about the title. Reality caught up with me at lightning speed, but some memories of Berlin have remained. The open-top bus, Helene Fischer on stage, Paul Kalkbrenner in the midst of it all. Each of the four camp houses put on a little show. None of it was coordinated; it all came out instinctively, and I think people could feel that. It was important to us to show our gratitude for all the support after those many bittersweet near victories and to share our success with the fans. And it was crucial to actually be able to present the trophy in the end, symbolically vanquishing all of the criticisms of the past ten years.

There's a lack of leadership. There aren't any characters. That side can only play pretty, but they can't win. All of that stuff would have been brought back up had we returned from Brazil empty-handed. Even my wife had given me a piece of advice before our departure. 'Without the Cup, you can't show your face around here again.' Whenever I spoke to him via FaceTime, my son Paul would cry bitter tears, because of how much he missed me. 'When are you finally coming home, Daddy?' It couldn't all be in vain. We had been sure we had shaken things up in Germany since 2004, quite a lot, actually. But not until we had won the title were we able to talk about success, about having reached our goal.

After the tournament, it was important to me to take a month to organise my thoughts and talk to people. It wasn't supposed to be a rushed decision made in a state of intoxication. But for the most part, everything was settled. After ten wonderful, extremely intense years with the national team, with over 100 caps and five major tournaments, I didn't want to wait for an end to this chapter. I wanted to decide it myself. I didn't want things to simply fizzle out the way it had happened to some other older players. I am proud and grateful to have been in the game for so long, to have been backed for so long. It was a golden ending, the most beautiful and emotional one you could imagine. In Brazil, the circle had closed. I didn't want to reopen it.

5

THE BEGINNING

IN THE SUMMER OF 2018, I TOOK CHARGE OF Arsenal's Academy. It's an exciting challenge, forming young players in a way that allows them to make the jump into the first team, stay there permanently, and play to their full potential. Unfortunately, even at a club like Arsenal, where the advancement of home-grown players is a priority since Arsène Wenger assumed office in 1996, this still works out for far too few. At the same time, we need to take care of the majority who fail to make it, for whom the step into professional football is too much for whatever reason. In England, sixty percent of all young professionals who sign a training contract at sixteen are out of a job two years later. That's the shocking reality. As a club, it is our responsibility to rescue these boys or, ideally, not allow it to come to that in the first place. Because even those youngsters seen as having outstanding potential only stand little chance of making a living off football; it's irresponsible to make their athletic education the only focus. We have to make life skills available to them, so that they may exist successfully in a world that doesn't put football at its centre.

In Germany, academy work was professionalised around the turn of the century. The centres for excellence, modelled on their English and French counterparts, were critical to our return to the top. Coaches and physios are highly specialised, training pitches are perfect, and the result is a large number of young players advancing thought the ranks. Personally, though, I was lucky to miss out on all of that at Hannover, who only established their academy when I was already with the Under-23s. If it had existed sooner, they would have culled me at thirteen, fourteen, or, at the very latest, during my injury phase at fifteen, and I would have never managed to come back. It's beyond dispute: in today's system, as a proven late-starter with a body height uncharacteristic for the game, I would certainly not have made it.

Nowadays, the selection process is much harsher. Players are assessed, thumbs go up or down. The total focus on someone's footballing performance starts a lot sooner; everything shifts ahead by a couple of years. Having an agent at thirteen, fourteen has become the norm. Some boys are even getting their own boot deal at that age, and some sixteen-year-olds already make half a million pounds a year as Premier League apprentices. One fifteen-year-old from Europe who recently signed with a London club was promised a two-million-pound salary on his next birthday. Everyone hopes to rear the next big star. From the clubs' point of view, money is virtually no object: there's enough of that around. Many who concern themselves with the fostering of youth players in England know that these sums are a problem. In the past, the formula for financial prosperity required success. The Premier League omits this first rung on the ladder: one can grow rich without ever playing a single game for the first team. The fact that this approach is poison for the sustainable, gradual development of young players is obvious. Some clubs are discussing whether to introduce a salary cap of £40,000 a year for teenagers. At the same time, though, there is concern that the competition wouldn't join in, but rather poach the best players instead. The rivalry between academies is great. People want to prove themselves to their superiors at the club, and the prospect of vast sums attracts agents and family members, who all want a piece of the action.

At the forefront, there are questions like 'How much can I make?' and, 'How much can I take away?' For some lower-income families, a child with a gift for football becomes a ticket for a better life. It's terrible when the natural order of things shifts this way and the child is suddenly responsible for the wellbeing of the parents. 'You need to make it, so that we're set for life. You have to support us.' The parents don't even need to say this out loud; a child can sense it. Suddenly, everything revolves around a teenager's wishes and interests, and if football doesn't work out, everything falls apart. So much pressure at such a young age can't be healthy. One can imagine how kids develop severe mental difficulties, being left with nothing at seventeen or eighteen. Now, the FA approaches the problem more aggressively, with career counselling and the offer of psychological help. But how many are willing to accept that they need this help? Are they able to admit to themselves that they won't make it after all? We cannot do enough here. Currently, the Robert Enke Foundation is in talks with the FA over extending its work to the UK.

I was fortunate to come from a middle-class home; no one pressured me to become a professional footballer. On the contrary, my parents wanted me to go to school, so, had things not worked out, I would have simply done something else to make a living. The big problem in England is that most of the boys at the academies leave school at sixteen and put all their eggs into one basket: footballer or nothing. Unlike in Germany, there are very few partnerships with schools that would enable young players to do their A-levels on the side. Instead, it's over for those kids after their GCSEs. They're subjected to so much training that there isn't time for an apprenticeship or further education. Arsenal's Academy makes their players attend a seminar in sports marketing. Twice a week, the kids click around a bit on a screen, and in the end, they get a diploma. But on the job market, that doesn't you get far.

That needs to change, for three reasons. First, we can't take away someone's childhood at sixteen and demand they devote every minute of every day to football. Second, it's far too risky to focus this early on a job which has such a poor prospect of long-term employment. I think often about the fact that no one else in my year at Hannover managed to establish themselves in professional football. No one, not even that major talent everyone kept hyping up. So much can happen at sixteen. You get injured, you're out. You can't keep up with the mental pace, you're out. You do something stupid, you're out. Or you stick with it until you're nineteen but then don't get a contract, because your club prefers to buy established players, and you're out. It can all be over from one day to the next. Third, it's a mistake to demand as little of young people, both mentally and in terms of organisation, as most of the academies do. As a youth player, you only need to turn up to training and follow the ball. A cab delivers you to the ground; you'll walk five metres at best. You don't need to take care of anything. Other people wash your things and carry your stuff to the pitch. You stare at your phone and post pictures to Instagram.

Most of the players would struggle massively to find their way to training if their cab failed to show on a given day. It would end in chaos and this lack of self-dependence is reflected by how they move around the pitch: disorientated. They can't react to anything unexpected, can't make autonomous decisions under pressure. Not without good reason does football pride itself on being a school for life: through fun and games, you learn to cooperate with people, to respect others regardless of their background, and to adhere to rules. But life is also a school for football. For my development as a limited player, daily training was less important than the ability to organise my daily routine, to reflect, to have a handle on my life.

What's my destination? How much more studying do I have to do? What kind of stuff do I need to take with me?

I wasn't exactly gifted, but I wasn't without talent. I knew how to deal with things. I could assess and process situations properly. Later on, that helped me to withstand greater stress, to beat my fear of failure, and to cope with the pressure of having sixty thousand people watching me. I know that complaints from senior generations about supposedly softening standards are as old as time. I don't want to glorify the past, either. It's good that certain macho rituals have died out and today's game is mostly considered just that and played as just that, rather than as a kind of war with a ball, military commanding structure included. Nevertheless, I'm convinced that it's counterproductive to remove all potential obstacles from the paths of young players at the outset, to relieve them of all their external tasks, in order to stick them inside a hermetically sealed world.

At Arsenal, I am trying to create an environment which not only supports these kids but challenges them, both on and off the pitch. I want them to be confronted with normality, to learn life lessons alongside game play and formations. Football mustn't be the only purpose in the life of a sixteen-year-old human being. Reversing this status quo requires an incredible number of people committed to the challenge, people who know from experience how important it is not to lose yourself in this talent spiel and to be able to brace yourself for a bumpy ride. Mirko Slomka meant well after all when he said it wasn't a foul all those years ago. You have to be able to cope with certain things. Life isn't always fair: the world's best footballer might never win the

World Cup. Instead, he had to watch some blonde beanpole, who should have stuck to swimming, leave the Maracanã with the trophy. Anything's possible.

ACKNOWLEDGEMENTS

BOOKS ACCOMPANIED ME THROUGHOUT MY PLAYING career. They were my stimulus and my hiatus on many trips, during long hours spent in hotels, and at countless tournaments. Back then, the thought of writing one myself didn't occur to me. Towards the end of my career, however, I nurtured a desire to reflect on and write down those past years. A kind of self-contemplation, a processing of an incredible period in my life — that Pattensen lad really won the World Cup. Utter madness.

A project like this comes into being though trust and team spirit, and I would like to express my gratitude to my teammates:

My wife, Ulrike, for the editing and emotional support;

My family in Pattensen for the assistance in reappraising the content and imagery of my childhood and my youth;

Raphael Honigstein for his calm and curiosity during the task of putting my story and my thoughts into words;

My German publisher, Ullstein Verlag, for their excellent co-operation from start to finish;

My agency, Spielerrat, for their professional and trusting support;

and, of course, you, dear reader.

Per

STATISTICS & CAREER NOTES

HANNOVER 96

2003/04
DFB-Pokal
Appearances: 1

Bundesliga
Appearances: 13

2004/05
DFB-Pokal
Appearances: 4
Goals: 1

Bundesliga
Appearances: 31
Goals: 2

2005/06

DFB-Pokal
Appearances: 3

Bundesliga
Appearances: 30
Goals: 5

TOTAL
DFB-Pokal
Appearances: 8
Goals: 1

Bundesliga
Appearances: 74
Goals: 7

OVERALL TOTAL
Appearances: 82
Goals: 8

WERDER BREMEN

2006/07

Bundesliga
Appearances: 25 (1)
Goals: 2

Europa League
Appearances: 5
Goals: 1

Champions League
Appearances: 5
Goals: 1

DFL-Ligapokal
Appearances: 1

2007/08

DFB-Pokal
Appearances: 3

Bundesliga
Appearances: 32
Goals: 1

Europa League
Appearances: 4

Champions League qualification
Appearances: 2

Champions League
Appearances: 5

2008/09

DFB-Pokal
Appearances: 3
Goals: 1

Bundesliga
Appearances: 23
Goals: 2

Europa League
Appearances: 7

Champions League
Appearances: 6
Goals: 1

2009/10

DFB-Pokal
Appearances: 6

Bundesliga
Appearances: 33
Goals: 5

Europa League qualification
Appearances: 2

Europa League
Appearances: 10

2010/11
DFB-Pokal
Appearances: 2

Bundesliga
Appearances: 30
Goals: 2

Champions League qualification
Appearances: 2

Champions League
Appearances: 5

2011/12
Bundesliga
Appearances: 4
Goals: 0

TOTAL

Bundesliga	DFB-Pokal
Appearances: 147 (1)	Appearances: 14
Goals: 12	Goals: 1

DFB Liga-Pokal	Europa League Qualification
Appearances: 1	Appearances: 2

Europa League
Appearances: 26
Goals: 1

Champions League
Appearances: 21
Goals: 2

OVERALL TOTAL
Appearances: 215 (1)
Goals: 16

Champions League qualification
Appearances: 4

ARSENAL

2011/12
FA Cup
Appearances: 1

Premier League
Appearances: 21

Champions League
Appearances: 5

2012/13
League Cup
Appearances: 1

FA Cup
Appearances: 3

Premier League
Appearances: 34 (1)
Goals: 3

Champions League
Appearances: 6

2013/14

League Cup
Appearances: 1

FA Cup
Appearances: 6 (1)
Goals: 1

Premier League
Appearances: 35
Goals: 2

Champions League qualification
Appearances: 2

Champions League
Appearances: 8

2014/15

FA Cup
Appearances: 4
Goals: 2

Premier League
Appearances: 35

Champions League qualification
Appearances: 1

Champions League
Appearances: 8

2015/16

Community Shield
Appearances: 1

League Cup
Appearances: 2

FA Cup
Appearances: 3

Premier League
Appearances: 24

Champions League
Appearances: 6 (1)

2016/17
FA Cup
Appearances: 1

Premier League
Appearances: 1 (1)

2017/18
Community Shield
Appearances: 1

League Cup
Appearances: 1

FA Cup
Appearances: 1
Goals: 1

Premier League
Appearances: 6 (2)
Goals: 1

Europa League
Appearances: 3

TOTAL

Premier League
Appearances: 156 (4)
Goals: 6

League Cup
Appearances: 5

FA Cup
Appearances: 19 (1)
Goals: 4

Community Shield
Appearances: 2

Champions League qualification
Appearances: 3

Champions League
Appearances: 33 (1)

Europa League
Appearances: 3

OVERALL TOTAL

Appearances: 221 (7)
Goals: 10

GERMANY

2004

Friendly
Appearances: 4 (1)

2005

Friendly
Appearances: 9

Confederations Cup
Appearances: 5
Goals: 1

2006
Friendly
Appearances: 5 (1)

World Cup
Appearances: 6

2007
Friendly
Appearances: 2

European Championship qualifiers
Appearances: 8

2008
Friendly
Appearances: 5

World Cup qualifiers
Appearances: 2

European Championships
Appearances: 6

2009
Friendly
Appearances: 2

World Cup qualifiers
Appearances: 5

2010
Friendly
Appearances: 3

World Cup
Appearances: 7

European Championship qualifiers
Appearances: 4

2011
Friendly
Appearances: 3

European Championship qualifiers
Appearances: 3

2012
Friendly
Appearances: 3

World Cup qualifiers
Appearances: 3
Goals: 1

2013
Friendly
Appearances: 5
Goals: 1

World Cup qualifiers
Appearances: 5
Goals: 1

2014
Friendly
Appearances: 3

World Cup
Appearances: 6 (2)

TOTAL

Friendly
Appearances: 44 (2)
Goals: 1

Confederations Cup
Appearances: 5
Goals: 1

European Championships qualifiers
Appearances: 15

European Championships
Appearances: 6

World Cup qualifiers
Appearances: 15
Goals: 2

World Cup
Appearances: 19 (2)

OVERALL TOTAL
Appearances: 104
Goals: 4

CAREER NOTES

HANNOVER 96

2003/04

Per Mertesacker was handed his debut at the club he had grown up at in November 2003 in a Bundesliga match against Cologne by the legendary coach Ralf Rangnick. At the time of his debut he was the youngest German-born player in the Bundesliga. Though he played out of position at right-back on his debut, he would go on to feature 13 times in the league that campaign.

2004/05

By the 2004/05 season, Mertesacker had become a regular in the heart of Hannover's defence, and scored his first professional goal in August 2004 with a last-minute equaliser against Borussia Dortmund. His performances at such a young age were enough to capture the attention of Germany manager Jürgen Klinsmann, who handed him his international debut in a friendly against Iran in November. Under new manager Ewald Lienen, Hannover finished the season in a respectable tenth place.

2005/06

With Germany hosting the World Cup in the summer of 2006, this campaign was a crucial one for the defender. In November Hannover once again replaced their manager in mid-season, with Peter Neuruer replacing Lienen, but Mertesacker remained a constant in the team and started to find his goalscoring touch too, netting five times in the Bundesliga. His club side limped to a twelfth place finish, but his performances in football's biggest showpiece that summer hinted at bigger things to come.

WERDER BREMEN

2006/07

Not long after Germany had captured the nation's imagination in reaching the semi-finals of the World Cup, Mertesacker made the short trip up north to Bremen in a move worth €5 million. Under the innovative Thomas Schaaf Bremen had won the Bundesliga in the 2003/04 campaign, and the step up in standard was reflected by the fact that he was now playing Champions League football, scoring the winner against Chelsea in November 2006.

2007/08

In the 2007/08 campaign Bremen once again competed in Europe's premier cub competition, and were Bayern's closest challengers in the league, finishing 10 points behind the Bavarian giants. Mertesacker featured 32 times in the Bundesliga, more than he ever had done before, and also 11 times in European competition. Bremen dropped into the UEFA Cup after finishing third in their Champions League group, but were knocked out in the last 16 by eventual finalists Glasgow Rangers.

2008/09

The 2008/09 season was Per's most exciting and successful season to date. Though Schaaf's team slipped way down to tenth in the Bundesliga, they had two cup competitions to focus on. In the space of around two weeks in April and May they faced Hamburg on three occasions, twice in the semi-final of the UEFA Cup and once in the DFB-Pokal semi-final. They were victorious in the German Cup via a penalty shootout, and though Mertesacker was injured in the second leg of the UEFA Cup away from home, they prevailed in that as well. Bremen beat Bayer Leverkusen 1-0 in the DFB-Pokal final but came unstuck in Istanbul, losing 2-1 to Shakhtar Donetsk, denying them their first UEFA Cup victory.

2009/10

Bremen's mid-table finish in the 2008/09 campaign and their failure to win the UEFA Cup at the end of the last campaign meant there was no European football this season, though there was a World Cup at the end of the summer to work towards. Mertesacker equalled his best goalscoring campaign in professional football with five strikes, as Bremen finished in a respectable third. Mertesacker was a regular in South Africa in that summer and featured in Germany's 4-1 victory over England, though they were once again undone by Spain in the semi-finals, just like in the 2008 European Championships.

2010/11

The 2010/11 season would be Per's last full campaign in German club football, but with Bremen continuing to lose players to bigger clubs, such as Mesut Özil who joined Madrid after the World

Cup, it was a tough one, and they finished in 13th. Mertesacker was once again a regular in the team, but by the end of the campaign it was time for him to make a fresh start.

ARSENAL

2011/12

It initially seemed as if Per's move away from Bremen was not going to happen that summer, and he played four Bundesliga games at the start of the 2011/12 campaign, but when Arsenal lost 8-2 at Manchester United early in the same season, Arsène Wenger came calling. Coming straight into the team he had to adapt quickly to his new surroundings in English football, as Arsenal recovered to finish in third.

2012/13

The 2012/13 campaign saw Mertesacker and Arsenal face German opponents Schalke 04 in the Champions League group stage and after finishing second they were handed a tie against the daunting Bayern Munich in the next round. After losing the home leg 3-1 they recovered brilliantly to win 2-0 in the Allianz arena, but cruelly exited on away goals. Bayern would go on to beat Borussia Dortmund in an all-German final, while Arsenal once again finished in the top four to ensure Champions League football.

2013/14

After an opening day defeat to Aston Villa, the Gunners were on fine form at the start of this campaign, winning 11 of their next 13 games thereafter to give them a shot at the league going into the new year. Their form tailed off particularly in February and March, but they kept their FA Cup run going and eventually sealed the title in dramatic circumstances, coming from two goals down against Hull City to win 3-2 at Wembley, giving Mertesacker his first trophy in England and Arsenal's first since the Invincibles won the league in 2003/04. Mertesacker topped off the summer in spectacular fashion, winning his first and only major honour with his country as Germany's golden generation finally tasted success after defeating hosts Brazil 7-1 in the semi-final and Argentina in the final to taste World Cup glory for the first time since 1990.

2014/15

In this campaign Arsenal did not have to face Bayern Munich in the Champions League round of sixteen for a third season in a row but were still defeated at the same stage by surprise package Monaco. The Gunners did not mount a significant challenge in the Premier League, but completed an FA Cup double with a more comfortable victory this time, Mertesacker getting his first goal in a major final in a 4-0 win over Aston Villa.

2015/16

With all the other big teams going through transitional periods, Arsenal had a real opportunity to win the Premier League for the first time in over ten years, and they looked to be in a good position to do so when a late Danny Welbeck goal gave them a

2-1 over surprise title rivals Leicester in February. Once again though, the Gunners' form tailed off and the Foxes held their nerve to become the most unlikely winners in the competition's history. Arsenal did pip Spurs to second place, meaning they had finished above their rivals in every season since Mertesacker had arrived at the club.

2016/17

This was a campaign of frustration for Mertesacker, as due to injury he played only one game in the Premier League as Arsenal finally failed to qualify for the Champions League, the club finishing outside the top four for the first time since the 1995/96 campaign. But due to a spate of injuries in defence, Per returned to the Arsenal backline to face champions Chelsea in the FA Cup, and a masterful performance against the brilliant Diego Costa in attack saw him win his third FA Cup title with the club, Wenger's last success with Arsenal.

2017/18

The 2017/18 campaign was a season of goodbyes at the Emirates, as Wenger finally departed after being at the helm since 1996. It was also the end of the road for Per in professional football, after 15 years in the game and 221 games with the Gunners. Arsenal would reach the semi-finals of the Europa League, but lost on aggregate to eventual champions Atlético Madrid.